Place Value

3-4

Written by

Denise Skomer

Editor: Collene Dobelmann
Illustrator: Ann Iosa
Production: Carrie Rickmond
Cover Designer: Barbara Peterson
Art Director: Moonhee Pak
Project Manager: Collene Dobelmann
Project Director: Betsy Morris

Table of Contents

Introduction

Each book in the *Power Practice*™ series contains dozens of ready-to-use activity pages to provide students with skill practice. These fun, engaging activities can be used to supplement and enhance what you are already teaching in your classroom. Give an activity page to students as independent class work, or send the pages home as homework to reinforce skills taught in class. An answer key is provided at the end of the book for quick reference.

Place Value 3–4 provides activities that will directly assist students in developing a strong foundation for number and operations skills

such as grouping, addition, subtraction, multiplication, division, decimals, greater than, less than, and more!

This book is divided into five main sections: Base Ten Blocks, Number Names, Decimals, More or Less, and Operations. You will find a variety of activity pages in each section that will reinforce math skills and build fluency with each concept.

Use these ready-to-go activities to "recharge" skill review and give students the power to succeed!

Hundreds, Tens, and Ones

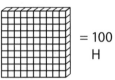 = 100
H

= 10
T

= 1
O

Write the number of hundreds, tens, and ones. Then write the number.

1
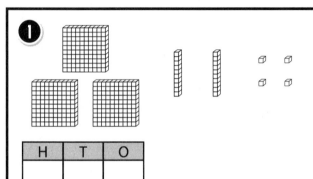

H	T	O

Number _____

2
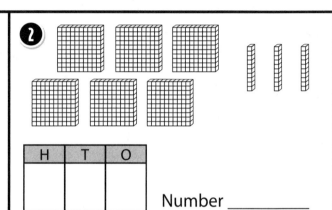

H	T	O

Number _____

3

H	T	O

Number _____

4
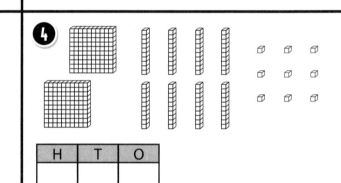

H	T	O

Number _____

5
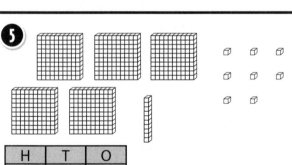

H	T	O

Number _____

6
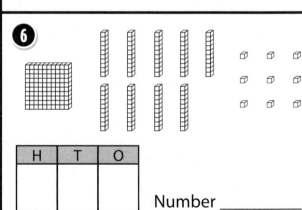

H	T	O

Number _____

Place Value • 3–4 © 2007 Creative Teaching Press

More Hundreds, Tens, and Ones

Write the number of hundreds, tens, and ones. Then write the number.

1

H	T	O

Number _____

2

H	T	O

Number _____

3

H	T	O

Number _____

4

H	T	O

Number _____

5

H	T	O

Number _____

6

H	T	O

Number _____

7

H	T	O

Number _____

8

H	T	O

Number _____

Place Value • 3–4 © 2007 Creative Teaching Press

Thousands

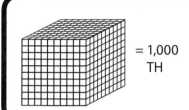

= 1,000
TH

= 100
H

= 10
T

= 1
O

Write the number of thousands, hundreds, tens, and ones. Then write the number.

①

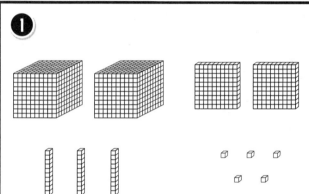

TH	H	T	O

Number _____

②

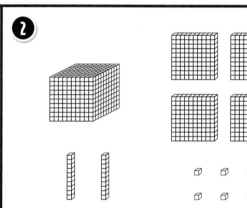

TH	H	T	O

Number _____

③

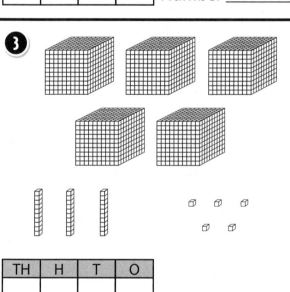

TH	H	T	O

Number _____

④

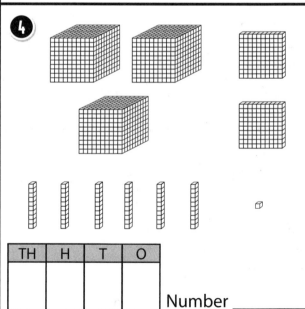

TH	H	T	O

Number _____

Place Value • 3–4 © 2007 Creative Teaching Press

More Thousands

Write the number of thousands, hundreds, tens, and ones. Then write the number.

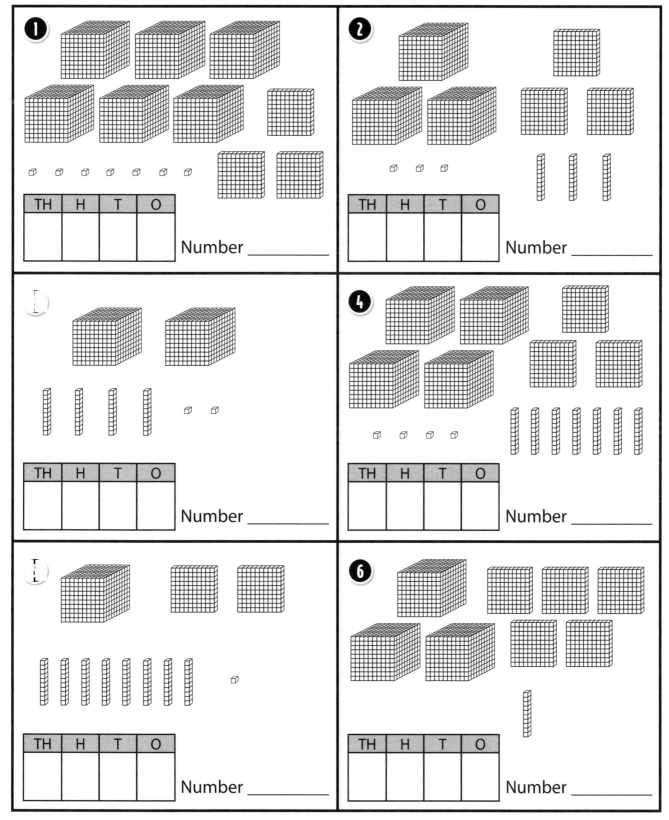

1

TH	H	T	O

Number _____

2

TH	H	T	O

Number _____

3

TH	H	T	O

Number _____

4

TH	H	T	O

Number _____

5

TH	H	T	O

Number _____

6

TH	H	T	O

Number _____

Place Value • 3–4 © 2007 Creative Teaching Press

Name _____. _____ Date _____

Mix It Up

Write the number for each mixed-up set of base ten blocks.

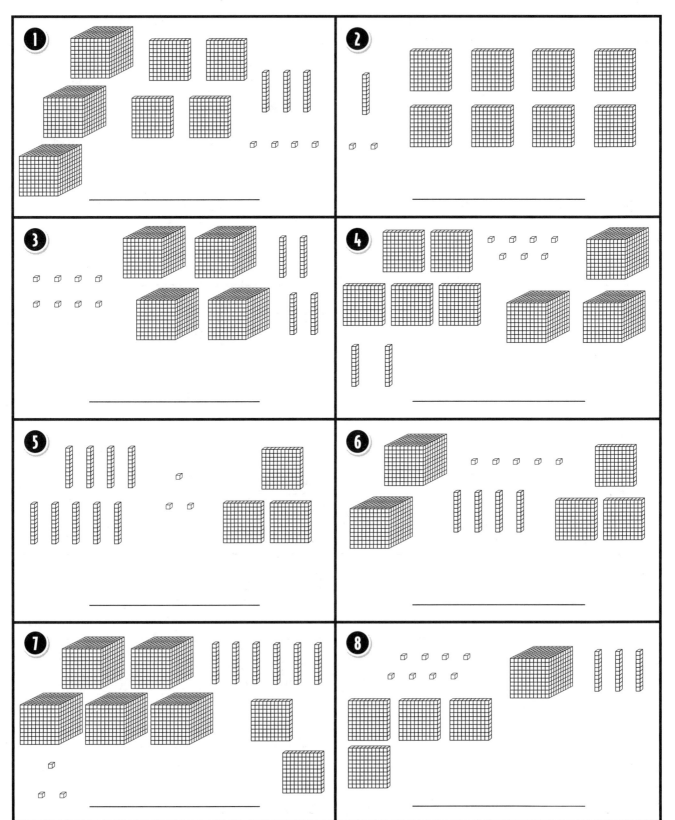

Place Value • 3–4 © 2007 Creative Teaching Press

Star Power

Color the star that shows the number for each set of base ten blocks.

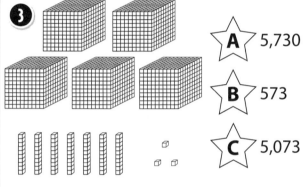

1
A 3,227
B 2,237
C 2,327

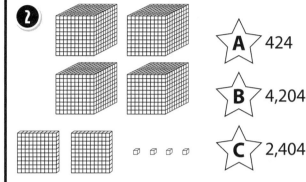

2
A 424
B 4,204
C 2,404

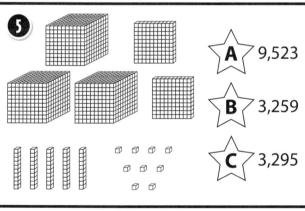

3
A 5,730
B 573
C 5,073

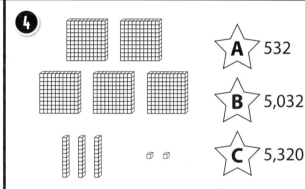

4
A 532
B 5,032
C 5,320

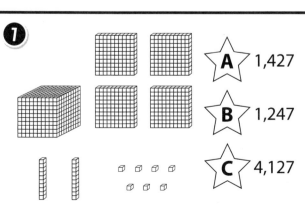

5
A 9,523
B 3,259
C 3,295

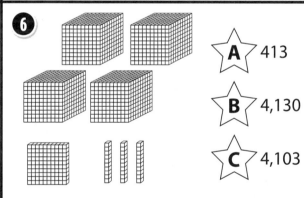

6
A 413
B 4,130
C 4,103

7
A 1,427
B 1,247
C 4,127

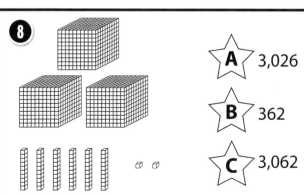

8
A 3,026
B 362
C 3,062

What's the Value?

millions	hundred thousands	ten thousands	thousands	hundreds	tens	ones
2 ,	3	4	5 ,	6	7	8

Find the 7 in each number. Write the place value name. The first one is done for you.

1 2,731

hundreds
_____

2 741

_____

3 67,891

_____

4 2,732,843

_____

5 417

_____

6 9,732

_____

7 79,342

_____

8 2,371

_____

9 47,368

_____

10 7,231,123

_____

11 2,719,243

_____

12 17

_____

Place Value • 3–4 © 2007 Creative Teaching Press

X Marks the Spot

 4,⨉36 ─────────────→ 8 is the largest digit.

It has a value of 800.

Draw an "X" on the largest digit. Write the digit's value.

1) 5,392

_____

2) 9,743,281

_____

3) 67,231

_____

4) 4,931

_____

5) 789

_____

6) 2,341

_____

7) 1,643,233

_____

8) 431

_____

9) 17,831

_____

10) 17,531

_____

11) 2,001,001

_____

12) 581,732

_____

Number Puzzler

Use all the numbers in each set to make the largest possible number. Use all of the numbers again to make the smallest possible number. (Zero cannot be used as the first digit.)

❶ (8, 3, 9, 2, 1)

_____ _____
largest   smallest

❷ (4, 9, 0, 1)

_____ _____
largest   smallest

❸ (3, 4, 7, 2, 2, 1)

_____ _____
largest   smallest

❹ (6, 3, 8, 1)

_____ _____
largest   smallest

❺ (4, 5, 1, 0, 2)

_____ _____
largest   smallest

❻ (7, 4, 3, 2, 1, 1, 0)

_____ _____
largest   smallest

❼ (5, 7, 6, 8)

_____ _____
largest   smallest

❽ (2, 1, 9, 0, 6)

_____ _____
largest   smallest

Place Value • 3–4 © 2007 Creative Teaching Press

Name That Number

Write the number in standard notation.

1 four hundred eighty-nine

_____

2 seven thousand, two hundred nine

_____

3 eighty-three thousand, four hundred seventy-one

_____

4 one million, two hundred forty-three thousand, two hundred twenty-one

_____

5 nine hundred forty-four

_____

6 two thousand, nine hundred twenty-three

_____

7 six hundred forty-two thousand, eight hundred seventy-three

_____

8 three thousand, four

_____

9 six thousand, nine hundred twenty

_____

10 fifty-two thousand, fifty-one

_____

11 seventy-two

_____

12 nine thousand, nine hundred ninety-nine

_____

Place Value • 3–4 © 2007 Creative Teaching Press

Expanding Numbers

Expanded Notation

12,345 = 10,000 + 2,000 + 300 + 40 + 5

Write each number in expanded notation.

1 7,283 = _____ + _____ + _____ + _____

2 15,039 = _____ + _____ + _____ + _____ + _____

3 298 = _____ + _____ + _____

4 37,384 = _____ + _____ + _____ + _____ + _____

5 4,807 = _____ + _____ + _____ + _____

6 60,936 = _____ + _____ + _____ + _____ + _____

7 989 = _____ + _____ + _____

8 4,568 = _____ + _____ + _____ + _____

Place Value • 3–4 © 2007 Creative Teaching Press

Numbers to Words

5,732 = five thousands + seven hundreds + three tens + two ones

Rewrite the numbers in expanded notation using number words.

1 257 = _____

2 3,807 = _____

3 14,291 = _____

4 7,340 = _____

5 1,098 = _____

6 31,783 = _____

7 5,494 = _____

8 682 = _____

Words to Numbers

two thousands + five hundreds + eight tens + four ones = 2,584

Rewrite the numbers in standard notation.

1 one ten thousand + five thousands +

four hundreds + three tens + two ones = _____

2 seven thousands + five hundreds + eight tens + three ones = _____

3 eight thousands + two hundreds + seven tens = _____

4 four hundreds + nine ones = _____

5 seven ten thousands + three hundreds + nine tens + two ones = _____

6 nine hundreds + eight tens + seven ones = _____

7 four thousands + four tens + five ones = _____

8 two ten thousands + eight thousands +

four hundreds + five tens + eight ones = _____

Place Value • 3–4 © 2007 Creative Teaching Press

Write It Out

Remember to hyphenate numbers when necessary.

Examples:
556 = five hundred fifty-six

81,408 = eighty-one thousand, four hundred eight

Write the word form for each number.

1) 432 = _____

2) 1,037 = _____

3) 22,345 = _____

4) 91,210 = _____

5) 18,123 = _____

6) 5,682 = _____

7) 9,069 = _____

8) 50,044 = _____

Number Riddles

Solve the number riddles. Circle the correct answers.

① The digit with the smallest value is 3. There are four hundreds. What is the number?

21,451   28,353   37,453

② There are seven thousands and two tens. The number is odd. What is the number?

17,563   17,321   17,122

③ The digit with the smallest value is a 9. There are three hundreds and four thousands. What is the number?

4,329   3,329   5,333

④ There are 4 ten thousands, five hundreds, and three ones. The number has one ten. What is the number?

43,513   42,522   43,503

⑤ The digit in the tens place is 7. There are four hundreds and nine ones. What is the number?

5,479   749   477

⑥ The number has four tens, three thousands, and two hundreds. The number is odd. What is the number?

13,240   4,321   3,241

⑦ There are 6 ten thousands and four hundreds. The digit in the thousands place and the digit in the hundreds place are the same. What is the number?

69,556   60,405   64,405

⑧ There are nine thousands in the number. The digit in the ones place is one more than the digit in the tens place. What is the number?

9,543   9,534   8,435

⑨ There are two hundreds, three ones, and six thousands. The digit in the ten thousands place is odd. What is the number?

46,293   24,203   16,213

⑩ The digit with the largest value is 1. There are nine thousands and seven tens. The number is even. What is the number?

4,319   19,872   19,879

Place Value • 3–4 © 2007 Creative Teaching Press

Name _____ Date _____

Base Ten Decimals

 = 1 whole   = ¹⁄₁₀ or 0.1   = ¹⁄₁₀₀ or 0.01

Base ten blocks can also be used to show decimals. A flat equals one whole. It can be broken into ten rods, each equaling one tenth of the whole. A rod can be broken into ten blocks, each equaling one hundredth of the flat.

Write the decimal number for each set of blocks.

❶ Number _____. _____ _____	**❷** 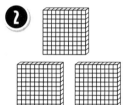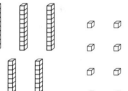 Number _____. _____ _____
❸ 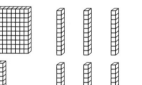 Number _____. _____ _____	**❹** 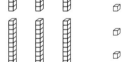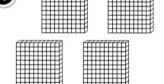 Number _____. _____ _____
❺ 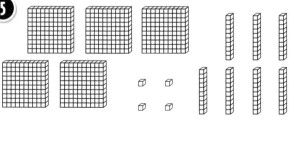 Number _____. _____ _____	**❻** 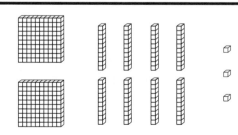 Number _____. _____ _____

Decimal Values

thousands	hundreds	tens	ones	decimal	tenths	hundredths
2 ,	6	5	4	.	3	8

The decimal point separates parts from the whole. When reading a decimal that is greater than 1, say the word **and** in place of the decimal point.

Example: The number 2,654.38 would be read as two thousand, six hundred fifty-four **and** thirty-eight hundredths.

Write the number using a decimal point.

1 five tenths

_____

2 two hundred fourteen and four tenths

_____

3 six and forty-three hundredths

_____

4 twenty-eight and three hundredths

_____

5 two thousand, four hundred nineteen and twenty-eight hundredths

_____

6 thirteen and thirteen hundredths

_____

7 fifty and six hundredths

_____

8 seventy-nine and eight hundredths

_____

9 twelve and eighty-three hundredths

_____

10 twelve hundredths

_____

11 fifty-one and sixty-three hundredths

_____

12 seven hundred eighty-one and three tenths

_____

Place Value • 3–4 © 2007 Creative Teaching Press

Name the Place Value

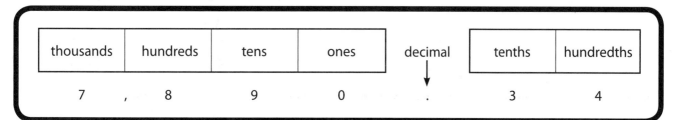

thousands	hundreds	tens	ones	decimal	tenths	hundredths
7 ,	8	9	0	.	3	4

Find the 5 in each number. Write the place value name. The first one is done for you.

1 243.51

_____tenths_____

2 5,732.8

_____

3 231.05

_____

4 351.89

_____

5 725.36

_____

6 8,345.71

_____

7 297.45

_____

8 391.52

_____

9 573.01

_____

10 372.85

_____

11 5,371.09

_____

12 282.57

_____

Doggone Decimals

When you read **tenths** or **hundredths**, you know those digits come after the decimal point.

Example: 57 hundredths = 0.57

Write the number in standard notation.

1 6 hundredths

_____0.06_____

2 4 tenths

_____

3 11 hundredths

_____

4 36 hundredths

_____

5 7 hundredths

_____

6 3 tenths

_____

7 4 hundredths

_____

8 75 hundredths

_____

9 13 hundredths

_____

10 8 tenths

_____

Circle the correct way to read each number.

11 0.18   eighteen tenths

eighteen hundredths

12 0.06   six tenths

six hundredths

13 0.43   forty-three tenths

forty-three hundredths

14 0.9   nine tenths

nine hundredths

Place Value • 3–4 © 2007 Creative Teaching Press

Spell It Out

Remember, **and** replaces the decimal point when we say, or write in word form, numbers that include both whole and fractional parts.

4.63 = four and sixty-three hundredths

Rewrite the following numbers in word form.

1) 4.71

_____

2 0.36

_____

3) 2.09

_____

4 21.7

_____

5 14.08

_____

6 9.79

_____

7) 210.1

_____

8 3.89

_____

9 17.4

_____

10 13.69

_____

11 9.08

_____

12 41.07

_____

Write It Out with Decimals

Rewrite the following numbers in word form.

1) 43.21 = _____

2) 1,007.05 = _____

3) 2,345.00 = _____

4) 3,210.9 = _____

5) 8,003.11 = _____

6) 600.29 = _____

7) 69.43 = _____

8) 50,000.7 = _____

Place Value • 3–4 © 2007 Creative Teaching Press

Money Matters

 one dollar and eleven cents = $1.11

Write each dollar amount using standard notation.

1) four dollars and thirty-two cents

$_____._____

2 seventy-three cents

$_____._____

3) fourteen dollars and seven cents

$_____._____

4 twelve dollars and twenty-two cents

$_____._____

5) forty dollars and four cents

$_____._____

6 six dollars and twelve cents

$_____._____

7) one dollar and eighty-eight cents

$_____._____

8 eighteen cents

$_____._____

9) ninety-four dollars and two cents

$_____._____

10 eight cents

$_____._____

11) five dollars and thirty-eight cents

$_____._____

12 forty cents

$_____._____

More Money Matters

Write each dollar amount in word form.

1 $12.43

_____

2 $31.07

_____

3 $2.01

_____

4 $0.74

_____

5 $8.72

_____

6 $12.40

_____

7 $20.31

_____

8 $53.15

_____

9 $4.70

_____

10 $10.10

_____

11 $48.08

_____

12 $19.29

_____

What's in Your Wallet?

 $1.00 $0.25 $0.10 $0.05 $0.01

Write the amount of money each person has.

1) Sam has 5 dollars, 3 quarters, and 2 dimes. How much money does he have? _____	**2** Maria has 3 quarters, 1 nickel, and 5 pennies. How much money does she have? _____
3) Alex has 1 dollar, 4 dimes, 2 nickels, and 4 pennies. How much money does he have? _____	**4** Jose has 6 dimes, 1 nickel, and 5 pennies. How much money does he have? _____
5) Leah has 6 dollars, 3 quarters, and 8 pennies. How much money does she have? _____	**6** Anna has 2 quarters, 4 dimes, 1 nickel, and 3 pennies. How much money does she have? _____
7) Terrell has 8 dollars, 1 quarter, 5 dimes, 2 nickels, and 2 pennies. How much money does he have? _____	**8** Danielle has 2 dollars, 2 quarters, 4 nickels, and 9 pennies. How much money does she have? _____

Place Value • 3–4 © 2007 Creative Teaching Press

Number Order

Write the numbers that come before and after each number below.

1 _____ 76 _____   **2** _____ 256 _____   **3** _____ 899 _____

4 _____ 1,754 _____   **5** _____ 3,298 _____   **6** _____ 786 _____

7 _____ 1,896 _____   **8** _____ 6,555 _____   **9** _____ 8,999 _____

10 _____ 249 _____   **11** _____ 8,948 _____   **12** _____ 768 _____

13 _____ 4,000 _____   **14** _____ 4,976 _____   **15** _____ 6,497 _____

16 _____ 2,341 _____   **17** _____ 8,901 _____   **18** _____ 640 _____

Place Value • 3–4 © 2007 Creative Teaching Press

Skip Counting

Write the numbers ten less and ten more than the number shown.

1 _____ 38 _____

2 _____ 243 _____

3 _____ 101 _____

4 _____ 1,782 _____

5 _____ 21 _____

6 _____ 213 _____

7 _____ 709 _____

8 _____ 4,581 _____

9 _____ 89 _____

10 _____ 714 _____

11 _____ 687 _____

12 _____ 13 _____

Write the numbers one hundred less and one hundred more than the number shown.

13 _____ 482 _____

14 _____ 112 _____

15 _____ 7,321 _____

16 _____ 9,089 _____

17 _____ 721 _____

18 _____ 190 _____

19 _____ 2,431 _____

20 _____ 8,982 _____

21 _____ 276 _____

22 _____ 1,054 _____

23 _____ 857 _____

24 _____ 1,968 _____

Number Climbing

Write the numbers in order from least to greatest.

1 768; 786; 743; 792 _____

2 1,276; 1,381; 1,042; 1,277 _____

3 3,799; 3,801; 3,621; 3,810 _____

4 491; 472; 409; 503 _____

5 23,716; 2,761; 23,167; 21,001 _____

Write the numbers in order from greatest to least.

6 3,971; 3,871; 3,900; 3,089 _____

7 891; 889; 817; 904 _____

8 31,001; 31,100; 32,901; 31,010 _____

9 115; 121; 215; 191 _____

10 386; 357; 348; 368 _____

Place Value • 3–4 © 2007 Creative Teaching Press

Creepy Comparisons

Write > or < in each ◯ .

1 765 ◯ 756   **2** 2,918 ◯ 2,098   **3** 699 ◯ 996

4 556 ◯ 555   **5** 781 ◯ 871   **6** 334 ◯ 338

7 591 ◯ 519   **8** 9,008 ◯ 9,080   **9** 2,978 ◯ 2,798

10 1,000 ◯ 999   **11** 1,209 ◯ 1,999   **12** 7,001 ◯ 7,100

13 311 ◯ 310   **14** 777 ◯ 888   **15** 3,210 ◯ 1,230

16 1,678 ◯ 1,768   **17** 489 ◯ 429   **18** 670 ◯ 760

Place Value • 3–4 © 2007 Creative Teaching Press

Out-of-This-World Comparisons

Write >, <, or = in each ◯ .

1 789 ◯ 700 + 90 + 8

2 4,000 + 200 + 7 ◯ 4,027

3 8,000 + 400 + 30 + 1 ◯ 8,431

4 901 ◯ 900 + 10 + 1

5 7,899 ◯ 8,000 + 700 + 90 + 9

6 8,000 + 20 + 9 ◯ 892

7 988 ◯ 800 + 80 + 9

8 700 + 40 + 3 ◯ 743

9 9,092 ◯ 9,000 + 900 + 2

10 800 + 20 + 1 ◯ 801

11 972 ◯ 900 + 70 + 2

12 3,098 ◯ 300 + 80 + 9

Place Value • 3–4 © 2007 Creative Teaching Press

Name _____ Date _____

Wordy Comparisons

Write > or < in each ◯ .

1) fourteen ◯ forty

2) three hundred nine ◯ three hundred nineteen

3) five thousand, two hundred eighty-four ◯ five thousand, two hundred forty-eight

4) eighteen thousand, three ◯ eighteen thousand, thirty

5) eleven thousand, one hundred twenty-two ◯ eleven thousand, two hundred eleven

6) sixty-nine thousand, five hundred sixty ◯ sixty-nine thousand, five hundred six

7) one hundred ninety-nine ◯ one thousand, ninety-nine

8) thirty thousand ◯ thirteen thousand

9) seventeen thousand, nine hundred eighty-seven ◯ seventy-one thousand, nine hundred eighty-seven

10) six hundred twenty ◯ six hundred thirty-nine

11) four hundred fifty-eight ◯ four hundred eighty-five

12) twelve thousand, six ◯ six thousand, twelve

Place Value • 3–4 © 2007 Creative Teaching Press

Dive In and Compare

Write >, <, or = in each ◯ .

1 0.71 ◯ 0.17   **2** 1.93 ◯ 0.93   **3** 0.16 ◯ 0.60

4 0.60 ◯ 0.6   **5** 0.12 ◯ 0.31   **6** 0.9 ◯ 0.90

7 0.7 ◯ 0.82   **8** 0.48 ◯ 0.41   **9** 0.51 ◯ 0.52

10 0.87 ◯ 0.78   **11** 0.37 ◯ 0.39   **12** 0.6 ◯ 0.59

13 0.19 ◯ 0.31   **14** 0.68 ◯ 0.57   **15** 0.5 ◯ 0.50

16 0.36 ◯ 0.38   **17** 0.63 ◯ 0.8   **18** 0.4 ◯ 0.29

Place Value • 3–4 © 2007 Creative Teaching Press

Flowery Comparisons

Write > or < in each ( ).

1 1.21 ( ) 2.12   **2** 0.59 ( ) 1   **3** 2.38 ( ) 2.83

4 3.9 ( ) 3.19   **5** 27.1 ( ) 27.01   **6** 6.9 ( ) 6.91

7 14.4 ( ) 14.42   **8** 12.71 ( ) 12.8   **9** 90.91 ( ) 91.91

10 4.09 ( ) 4.9   **11** 14.7 ( ) 15   **12** 37.2 ( ) 37.19

13 0.75 ( ) 75   **14** 4.91 ( ) 4.9   **15** 18.8 ( ) 1.88

16 30.8 ( ) 30.38   **17** 7.29 ( ) 7.9   **18** 4.24 ( ) 4.44

Name _____ Date _____

Comparing Numbers and Words

Write >, <, or = in each 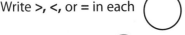.

1 3.34 ◯ three and thirty-four hundredths

2 0.89 ◯ eighty-nine

3 6.50 ◯ six hundred fifty

4 3.9 ◯ three and nine tenths

5 12.40 ◯ twelve and four hundredths

6 6.91 ◯ six and nineteen hundredths

7 192.55 ◯ one hundred ninety-nine

8 53.08 ◯ fifty-three and eight tenths

9 60.01 ◯ sixty and one hundredth

10 4.95 ◯ nine and forty-five hundredths

11 11.20 ◯ eleven and two tenths

12 3.00 ◯ three hundredths

13 999.99 ◯ one thousand

14 4.07 ◯ four and seven tenths

15 123.00 ◯ one hundred twenty-three

16 3.06 ◯ three and six hundredths

17 7.20 ◯ seven and two hundredths

18 0.45 ◯ four

Place Value • 3–4 © 2007 Creative Teaching Press

Comparing Prices

Circle the item that costs more.

1  $1.47 $1.74

2  $4.01 $4.10

3  $12.75 $21.75

4  $.94 $.90

5  $9.10 $9.90

6  $7.13 $7.31

Circle the item that costs less.

7  $48.29 $49.00

8  $1,290.99 $1,290.00

9  $75.02 $76.02

10  $17.82 $18.72

11  $0.73 $0.70

12  $14.77 $14.79

Place Value • 3–4 © 2007 Creative Teaching Press

Round and Round

When rounding to the nearest ten, look at the number in the ones place.
- If the number is less than 5, the tens place stays the same.   ⟶ 1<u>2</u> ⟶ 10
- If the number is 5 or greater, round up.   ⟶ 1<u>7</u> ⟶ 20

When rounding to the nearest hundred, look at the number in the tens place.
- If the number is less than 5, the hundreds place stays the same.   ⟶ 1<u>3</u>1 ⟶ 100
- If the number is 5 or greater, round up.   ⟶ 1<u>6</u>1 ⟶ 200

Round each number to the nearest ten.

1 73 _____   **2** 26 _____   **3** 143 _____

4 871 _____   **5** 987 _____   **6** 88 _____

7 74 _____   **8** 35 _____   **9** 458 _____

10 721 _____   **11** 81 _____   **12** 135 _____

Round each number to the nearest hundred.

13 240 _____   **14** 732 _____   **15** 581 _____

16 2,791 _____   **17** 1,891 _____   **18** 259 _____

19 179 _____   **20** 981 _____   **21** 435 _____

22 551 _____   **23** 648 _____   **24** 749 _____

Place Value • 3–4 © 2007 Creative Teaching Press

Round and Round Again

When rounding to the nearest whole number, look at the number in the tenths place.
- If the number is less than 5, the ones place stays the same. ⟶ 1.<u>2</u> ⟶ 1
- If the number is 5 or greater, round up. ⟶ 1.<u>6</u> ⟶ 2

When rounding to the nearest tenth, look at the number in the hundredths place.
- If the number is less than 5, the tenths places stays the same. ⟶ 1.2<u>1</u> ⟶ 1.2
- If the number is 5 or greater, round up. ⟶ 1.2<u>6</u> ⟶ 1.3

Round each number to the nearest whole number.

1 4.8 _____   **2** 7.6 _____   **3** 11.1 _____

4 43.6 _____   **5** 51.5 _____   **6** 124.4 _____

7 72.7 _____   **8** 23.5 _____   **9** 11.9 _____

10 36.5 _____   **11** 25.3 _____   **12** 8.9 _____

Round each number to the nearest tenth.

13 9.75 _____   **14** 30.21 _____   **15** 5.14 _____

16 38.68 _____   **17** 48.57 _____   **18** 71.16 _____

19 432.13 _____   **20** 13.62 _____   **21** 6.89 _____

22 42.85 _____   **23** 8.71 _____   **24** 17.48 _____

Regrouping Reminder

Addition
Add the ones.
Regroup the ones to make one more ten.
Then add the tens.

Tens	Ones
¹2	6
+1	6
4	2

Subtraction
Regroup the tens.
Add ten to the ones. Subtract.
Then subtract the tens.

Tens	Ones
²3̷	¹⁴4̷
−1	6
1	8

Add or subtract. Remember to regroup.

1 29
   +14
   ‾‾‾‾

2 36
   −18
   ‾‾‾‾

3 97
   −49
   ‾‾‾‾

4 28
   +39
   ‾‾‾‾

5 75
   +16
   ‾‾‾‾

6 68
   +23
   ‾‾‾‾

7 52
   −37
   ‾‾‾‾

8 19
   +17
   ‾‾‾‾

9 21
   −9
   ‾‾‾‾

10 58
   +39
   ‾‾‾‾

11 61
   −38
   ‾‾‾‾

12 57
   +37
   ‾‾‾‾

Three-Digit Addition and Subtraction— Regrouping

Addition
Add the ones. Regroup if needed.
Add the tens. Regroup if needed.
Then add the hundreds.

Hundreds	Tens	Ones
¹2	¹9	5
+1	2	7
4	2	2

Subtraction
Subtract the ones. Regroup the tens if needed.
Subtract the tens. Regroup the hundreds if needed.
Then subtract the hundreds.

Hundreds	Tens	Ones
³4̸	¹⁴5̸	¹⁴4̸
−2	8	6
1	6	8

Add or subtract. Regroup if needed.

    754
 − 387

2   423
 + 478

3   371
 − 218

4   728
 + 349

5   582
 − 371

6   814
 + 153

    713
 − 489

8   298
 + 198

9   638
 − 281

10   419
 + 290

11   500
 − 199

12   213
 + 689

Place Value • 3–4 © 2007 Creative Teaching Press

Multiplication Magic

Sometimes you need to regroup when multiplying. Multiply each digit of the top number by the bottom number. Regroup if the product is 10 or more.

Start with the ones place.

$$\begin{array}{r} {}^{1}15 \\ \times\ 3 \\ \hline 5 \end{array}$$

Then multiply the tens place, and add the regrouped number.

$$\begin{array}{r} {}^{1}15 \\ \times\ 3 \\ \hline 45 \end{array}$$

Multiply.

1
$$\begin{array}{r} 43 \\ \times\ 8 \\ \hline \end{array}$$

2
$$\begin{array}{r} 21 \\ \times\ 9 \\ \hline \end{array}$$

3
$$\begin{array}{r} 37 \\ \times\ 4 \\ \hline \end{array}$$

4
$$\begin{array}{r} 29 \\ \times\ 8 \\ \hline \end{array}$$

5
$$\begin{array}{r} 16 \\ \times\ 4 \\ \hline \end{array}$$

6
$$\begin{array}{r} 81 \\ \times\ 9 \\ \hline \end{array}$$

7
$$\begin{array}{r} 70 \\ \times\ 2 \\ \hline \end{array}$$

8
$$\begin{array}{r} 41 \\ \times\ 9 \\ \hline \end{array}$$

9
$$\begin{array}{r} 36 \\ \times\ 7 \\ \hline \end{array}$$

10
$$\begin{array}{r} 54 \\ \times\ 9 \\ \hline \end{array}$$

11
$$\begin{array}{r} 47 \\ \times\ 7 \\ \hline \end{array}$$

12
$$\begin{array}{r} 68 \\ \times\ 6 \\ \hline \end{array}$$

Place Value • 3–4 © 2007 Creative Teaching Press

Two-Digit Multiplication— Regrouping

Multiply each digit of the top number by the ones digit in the bottom number. Regroup if needed.

$$\begin{array}{r} 22 \\ \times 12 \\ \hline 44 \end{array}$$

On the next line, place a 0 in the ones place. Multiply each digit of the top number by the tens digit in the bottom number. Regroup if needed.

$$\begin{array}{r} 22 \\ \times 12 \\ \hline 44 \\ +220 \\ \hline \end{array}$$

Then add the products.

$$\begin{array}{r} 22 \\ \times 12 \\ \hline 44 \\ +220 \\ \hline 264 \end{array}$$

Multiply.

1 $\begin{array}{r} 41 \\ \times\ 18 \\ \hline \end{array}$

2 $\begin{array}{r} 23 \\ \times\ 15 \\ \hline \end{array}$

3 $\begin{array}{r} 30 \\ \times\ 17 \\ \hline \end{array}$

4 $\begin{array}{r} 44 \\ \times\ 24 \\ \hline \end{array}$

5 $\begin{array}{r} 55 \\ \times\ 12 \\ \hline \end{array}$

6 $\begin{array}{r} 31 \\ \times\ 21 \\ \hline \end{array}$

7 $\begin{array}{r} 13 \\ \times\ 16 \\ \hline \end{array}$

8 $\begin{array}{r} 11 \\ \times\ 23 \\ \hline \end{array}$

9 $\begin{array}{r} 32 \\ \times\ 25 \\ \hline \end{array}$

10 $\begin{array}{r} 16 \\ \times\ 10 \\ \hline \end{array}$

11 $\begin{array}{r} 20 \\ \times\ 49 \\ \hline \end{array}$

12 $\begin{array}{r} 22 \\ \times\ 28 \\ \hline \end{array}$

Name _____ Date _____

Division—No Remainders

| How many divisors are contained in the first digit of the dividend? $$\begin{array}{r} 1 \\ 4\overline{)72} \end{array}$$ | Multiply that number times the divisor. Take that answer and subtract it from the dividend. $$\begin{array}{r} 1 \\ 4\overline{)72} \\ -4 \\ \hline 3 \end{array}$$ | Bring down the next number in the dividend. How many divisors are contained in that number? Multiply and subtract. | $$\begin{array}{r} 1 \\ 4\overline{)72} \\ -4\downarrow \\ \hline 32 \\ -32 \\ \hline 0 \end{array}$$ |

1 $6\overline{)54}$ **2** $8\overline{)88}$ **3** $4\overline{)68}$ **4** $5\overline{)50}$

5 $7\overline{)98}$ **6** $8\overline{)24}$ **7** $5\overline{)110}$ **8** $8\overline{)336}$

9 $8\overline{)776}$ **10** $4\overline{)84}$ **11** $4\overline{)384}$ **12** $9\overline{)648}$

13 $2\overline{)98}$ **14** $4\overline{)104}$ **15** $3\overline{)108}$ **16** $2\overline{)28}$

44 Operations

Division 3–4 © 2007 Creative Teaching Press

Name _____ Date _____

Division–Remainders

A dividend does not always contain equal sets of the divisor. The amount not contained in a set is the **remainder**. The remainder will always be less than the divisor.

$$\begin{array}{r} 2\,r2 \\ 5\overline{)12} \\ -10 \\ \hline 2 \end{array}$$

1)
$$\begin{array}{r} 73\,r4 \\ 6\overline{)442} \\ -42 \\ \hline 22 \\ -18 \\ \hline 4 \end{array}$$

2) $9\overline{)48}$

3) $8\overline{)9}$

4) $5\overline{)902}$

5) $6\overline{)8}$

6) $8\overline{)57}$

7) $2\overline{)7}$

8) $5\overline{)839}$

9) $4\overline{)339}$

10) $9\overline{)59}$

11) $7\overline{)9}$

12) $2\overline{)5}$

13) $4\overline{)391}$

14) $8\overline{)451}$

15) $6\overline{)37}$

16) $5\overline{)18}$

Place Value • 3–4 © 2007 Creative Teaching Press

Answer Key

Hundreds, Tens, and Ones (page 4)

1. 3 hundreds, 2 tens, 4 ones; 324
2. 6 hundreds, 3 tens, 0 ones; 630
3. 4 hundreds, 0 tens, 6 ones; 406
4. 2 hundreds, 8 tens, 9 ones; 289
5. 5 hundreds, 1 ten, 8 ones; 518
6. 1 hundred, 9 tens, 9 ones; 199

More Hundreds, Tens, and Ones (page 5)

1. 4 hundreds, 4 tens, 1 one; 441
2. 5 hundreds, 1 ten, 5 ones; 515
3. 0 hundreds, 8 tens, 2 ones; 82
4. 3 hundreds, 2 tens, 8 ones; 328
5. 2 hundreds, 0 tens, 7 ones; 207
6. 7 hundreds, 1 ten, 0 ones; 710
7. 3 hundreds, 5 tens, 2 ones; 352
8. 4 hundreds, 5 tens, 6 ones; 456

Thousands (page 6)

1. 2 thousands, 2 hundreds, 3 tens, 5 ones; 2,235
2. 1 thousand, 4 hundreds, 2 tens, 8 ones; 1,428
3. 5 thousands, 0 hundreds, 3 tens, 5 ones; 5,035
4. 3 thousands, 2 hundreds, 6 tens, 1 one; 3,261

More Thousands (page 7)

1. 6 thousands, 3 hundreds, 0 tens, 7 ones; 6,307
2. 3 thousands, 3 hundreds, 3 tens, 3 ones; 3,333
3. 2 thousands, 0 hundreds, 4 tens, 2 ones; 2,042
4. 4 thousands, 3 hundreds, 7 tens, 4 ones; 4,374
5. 1 thousand, 2 hundreds, 8 tens, 1 one; 1,281
6. 3 thousands, 5 hundreds, 1 ten, 0 ones; 3,510

Mix It Up (page 8)

1. 3,434	**2.** 812
3. 4,048	**4.** 3,527
5. 393	**6.** 2,345
7. 5,263	**8.** 1,438

Star Power (page 9)

1. C	**2.** B
3. C	**4.** A
5. B	**6.** B
7. A	**8.** C

What's the Value? (page 10)

1. hundreds
2. hundreds
3. thousands
4. hundred thousands
5. ones
6. hundreds
7. ten thousands
8. tens
9. thousands
10. millions
11. hundred thousands
12. ones

X Marks the Spot (page 11)

1. 9; 90	**2.** 9; 9,000,000
3. 7; 7,000	**4.** 9; 900
5. 9; 9	**6.** 4; 40
7. 6; 600,000	**8.** 4; 400
9. 8; 800	**10.** 7; 7,000
11. 2; 2,000,000	**12.** 8; 80,000

Number Puzzler (page 12)

1. 98,321; 12,389
2. 9,410; 1,049
3. 743,221; 122,347
4. 8,631; 1,368
5. 54,210; 10,245
6. 7,432,110; 1,012,347
7. 8,765; 5,678
8. 96,210; 10,269

Name That Number (page 13)

1. 489	**2.** 7,209
3. 83,471	**4.** 1,243,221
5. 944	**6.** 2,923
7. 642,873	**8.** 3,004
9. 6,920	**10.** 52,051
11. 72	**12.** 9,999

Expanding Numbers (page 14)

1. 7,000 + 200 + 80 + 3
2. 10,000 + 5,000 + 0 + 30 + 9
3. 200 + 90 + 8
4. 30,000 + 7,000 + 300 + 80 + 4
5. 4,000 + 800 + 0 + 7
6. 60,000 + 0 + 900 + 30 + 6
7. 900 + 80 + 9
8. 4,000 + 500 + 60 + 8

Numbers to Words (page 15)

1. two hundreds + five tens + seven ones
2. three thousands + eight hundreds + seven ones
3. one ten thousand + four thousands + two hundreds + nine tens + one one
4. seven thousands + three hundreds + four tens
5. one thousand + nine tens + eight ones
6. three ten thousands + one thousand + seven hundreds + eight tens + three ones
7. five thousands + four hundreds + nine tens + four ones
8. six hundreds + eight tens + two ones

Words to Numbers (page 16)

1. 15,432
2. 7,583
3. 8,270
4. 409
5. 70,392
6. 987
7. 4,045
8. 28,458

Write It Out (page 17)

1. four hundred thirty-two
2. one thousand, thirty-seven
3. twenty-two thousand, three hundred forty-five
4. ninety-one thousand, two hundred ten
5. eighteen thousand, one hundred twenty-three
6. five thousand, six hundred eighty-two
7. nine thousand, sixty-nine
8. fifty thousand, forty-four

Number Riddles (page 18)

1. 37,453	**2.** 17,321
3. 4,329	**4.** 43,513
5. 5,479	**6.** 3,241
7. 64,405	**8.** 9,534
9. 16,213	**10.** 19,872

Base Ten Decimals (page 19)

1. 1.34	**2.** 3.58
3. 2.67	**4.** 4.09
5. 5.74	**6.** 2.83

Decimal Values (page 20)

1. 0.5
2. 214.4
3. 6.43
4. 28.03
5. 2,419.28
6. 13.13
7. 50.06
8. 79.08
9. 12.83
10. 0.12
11. 51.63
12. 781.3

Name the Place Value (page 21)

1. tenths
2. thousands
3. hundredths
4. tens
5. ones
6. ones
7. hundredths
8. tenths
9. hundreds
10. hundredths
11. thousands
12. tenths

Doggone Decimals (page 22)

1. 0.06
2. 0.4
3. 0.11
4. 0.36
5. 0.07
6. 0.3
7. 0.04
8. 0.75
9. 0.13
10. 0.8
11. eighteen hundredths
12. six hundredths
13. forty-three hundredths
14. nine tenths

Spell It Out (page 23)

1. four and seventy-one hundredths
2. thirty-six hundredths
3. two and nine hundredths
4. twenty-one and seven tenths
5. fourteen and eight hundredths
6. nine and seventy-nine hundredths
7. two hundred ten and one tenth
8. three and eighty-nine hundredths
9. seventeen and four tenths
10. thirteen and sixty-nine hundredths
11. nine and eight hundredths
12. forty-one and seven hundredths

Write It Out with Decimals (page 24)

1. forty-three and twenty-one hundredths
2. one thousand, seven and five hundredths
3. two thousand, three hundred forty-five
4. three thousand, two hundred ten and nine tenths
5. eight thousand, three and eleven hundredths
6. six hundred and twenty-nine hundredths
7. sixty-nine and forty-three hundredths
8. fifty thousand and seven tenths

Money Matters (page 25)

1. $4.32
2. $0.73
3. $14.07
4. $12.22
5. $40.04
6. $6.12
7. $1.88
8. $0.18
9. $94.02
10. $0.08
11. $5.38
12. $0.40

More Money Matters (page 26)

1. twelve dollars and forty-three cents
2. thirty-one dollars and seven cents
3. two dollars and one cent
4. seventy-four cents
5. eight dollars and seventy-two cents
6. twelve dollars and forty cents
7. twenty dollars and thirty-one cents
8. fifty-three dollars and fifteen cents
9. four dollars and seventy cents
10. ten dollars and ten cents
11. forty-eight dollars and eight cents
12. nineteen dollars and twenty-nine cents

What's in Your Wallet? (page 27)

1. $5.95
2. $0.85
3. $1.54
4. $0.70
5. $6.83
6. $0.98
7. $8.87
8. $2.79

Number Order (page 28)

1. 75; 77
2. 255; 257
3. 898; 900
4. 1,753; 1,755
5. 3,297; 3,299
6. 785; 787
7. 1,895; 1,897
8. 6,554; 6,556
9. 8,998; 9,000
10. 248; 250
11. 8,947; 8,949
12. 767; 769
13. 3,999; 4,001
14. 4,975; 4,977
15. 6,496; 6,498
16. 2,340; 2,342
17. 8,900; 8,902
18. 639; 641

Skip Counting (page 29)

1. 28; 48
2. 233; 253
3. 91; 111
4. 1,772; 1,792
5. 11; 31
6. 203; 223
7. 699; 719
8. 4,571; 4,591
9. 79; 99
10. 704; 724
11. 677; 697
12. 3; 23
13. 382; 582
14. 12; 212
15. 7,221; 7,421
16. 8,989; 9,189
17. 621; 821
18. 90; 290
19. 2,331; 2,531
20. 8,882; 9,082
21. 176; 376
22. 954; 1,154
23. 757; 957
24. 1,868; 2,068

Number Climbing (page 30)

1. 743 ; 768 ; 786 ; 792
2. 1,042 ; 1,276 ; 1,277 ; 1,381
3. 3,621 ; 3,799 ; 3,801 ; 3,810
4. 409 ; 472 ; 491 ; 503
5. 2,761 ; 21,001 ; 23,167 ; 23,716
6. 3,971 ; 3,900 ; 3,871 ; 3,089
7. 904 ; 891 ; 889 ; 817
8. 32,901 ; 31,100 ; 31,010 ; 31,001
9. 215 ; 191 ; 121 ; 115
10. 386 ; 368 ; 357 ; 348

Creepy Comparisons (page 31)

1. >
2. >
3. <
4. >
5. <
6. <
7. >
8. <
9. >
10. >
11. <
12. <
13. >
14. <
15. >
16. <
17. >
18. <

Out-of-This-World Comparisons (page 32)

1. <
2. >
3. =
4. <
5. <
6. >
7. >
8. =
9. <
10. >
11. =
12. >

Wordy Comparisons (page 33)

1. <
2. <
3. >
4. <
5. <
6. >
7. <
8. >
9. <
10. <
11. <
12. >

Dive In and Compare (page 34)

1. >
2. >
3. <
4. =
5. <
6. =
7. <
8. >
9. <
10. >
11. <
12. >
13. <
14. >
15. =
16. <
17. <
18. >

Flowery Comparisons (page 35)

1. <	2. <	3. <
4. >	5. >	6. <
7. <	8. <	9. <
10. <	11. <	12. >
13. <	14. >	15. >
16. >	17. <	18. <

Comparing Numbers and Words (page 36)

1. =	2. <	3. <	4. =
5. >	6. >	7. <	8. <
9. =	10. <	11. =	12. >
13. <	14. <	15. =	16. =
17. >	18. <		

Comparing Prices (page 37)

1. $1.74	2. $4.10
3. $21.75	4. $0.94
5. $9.90	6. $7.31
7. $48.29	8. $1,290.00
9. $75.02	10. $17.82
11. $0.70	12. $14.77

Round and Round (page 38)

1. 70	2. 30	3. 140
4. 870	5. 990	6. 90
7. 70	8. 40	9. 460
10. 720	11. 80	12. 140
13. 200	14. 700	15. 600
16. 2,800	17. 1,900	18. 300
19. 200	20. 1,000	21. 400
22. 600	23. 600	24. 700

Round and Round Again (page 39)

1. 5	2. 8	3. 11
4. 44	5. 52	6. 124
7. 73	8. 24	9. 12
10. 37	11. 25	12. 9
13. 9.8	14. 30.2	15. 5.1
16. 38.7	17. 48.6	18. 71.2
19. 432.1	20. 13.6	21. 6.9
22. 42.9	23. 8.7	24. 17.5

Regrouping Reminder (page 40)

1. 43	2. 18	3. 48
4. 67	5. 91	6. 91
7. 15	8. 36	9. 12
10. 97	11. 23	12. 94

Three-Digit Addition and Subtraction—Regrouping (page 41)

1. 367	2. 901	3. 153
4. 1,077	5. 211	6. 967
7. 224	8. 496	9. 357
10. 709	11. 301	12. 902

Multiplication Magic (page 42)

1. 344	2. 189	3. 148
4. 232	5. 64	6. 729
7. 140	8. 369	9. 252
10. 486	11. 329	12. 408

Two-Digit Multiplication—Regrouping (page 43)

1. 738	2. 345	3. 510
4. 1,056	5. 660	6. 651
7. 208	8. 253	9. 800
10. 160	11. 980	12. 616

Division—No Remainders (page 44)

1. 9	2. 11	3. 17	4. 10
5. 14	6. 3	7. 22	8. 42
9. 97	10. 21	11. 96	12. 72
13. 49	14. 26	15. 36	16. 14

Division—Remainders (page 45)

1. 73 r 4	2. 5 r 3	3. 1 r 1	4. 180 r 2
5. 1 r 2	6. 7 r 1	7. 3 r 1	8. 167 r 4
9. 84 r 3	10. 6 r 5	11. 1 r 2	12. 2 r 1
13. 97 r 3	14. 56 r 3	15. 6 r 1	16. 3 r 3

Fluency Builder

anxious	look	land
retire	plant	back
vacant	take	pass
sprucing	stand	spade
adore	see	amazed
recognizing	says	name
	what	gaze

1. This vacant lot / could use / some sprucing up.

2. My gram says / the name / of this flower.

3. I use / a spade / to plant / flowers and bulbs.

4. I am anxious to see / the beautiful flowers / grow.

5. Recognizing / different flowers / can be fun.

6. Take a look / at how pretty / the land looks now.

7. People pass by / just to gaze / at the pretty flowers.

8. They stand back / and adore / the flowers.

9. They are amazed / at what / they see!

Harcourt

Gram's Plant Parade

Read the story. Circle all the words with the short *a* vowel sound. Then draw a line under all the words with the long *a* vowel sound.

    Pam has a crate of canned hams. She likes ham with yams. In fact, now she craves some yams to go with her hams. She asks her dad for some. "We are all out, Pam. I will ask Wade if he has yams on his land."

    Wade has yams but no ham. Wade will trade some yams for a can of ham. He gets some fat yams out with the blade of his spade. Dad gets a ham. Then Dad and Wade make the trade.

    Dad takes the yams to Pam. She bakes the yams in a pan. She gets out some plates. Wade comes over and has some with her and her dad.

Now write the words with a short *a* or a long *a* vowel sound that best complete each sentence.

1. Pam likes to have _____ with her ham.

2. Her _____ asks Wade for yams.

3. Wade gets the yams out with his _____.

4. Pam's dad _____ a can of ham for some of the yams.

5. Pam _____ the yams and ham.

6. _____ comes over to have yams and ham with Pam.

Name _____

Gram's Plant Parade

Write one sentence in each box below to tell the main points of "Gram's Plant Parade."

Pages 6–7

Main Idea:

Pages 8–9

Main Idea:

Pages 10–11

Main Idea:

Now write a one-sentence summary about the story. Use the information from the boxes above.

_____

_____

_____

Narrative Elements

Read the paragraph and identify the narrative elements in the story.

Last summer, Adam and his grandpa went fishing at Blue Lake. Adam had never been fishing before. His grandpa taught him how to put a worm on his hook, throw out his line, and wait patiently for a nibble. Adam waited and waited. Finally, he felt a tug on the end of his pole. With the help of his grandpa, Adam landed his first fish. What an exciting day!

Setting

Characters

Plot

Harcourt

Fluency Builder

uneasy	things	smile
disappointment	your	pins
compromise	off	nine
perseverance	see	rides
leisure	hat	bike
chortle	can't	pigs
	when	six

1. Miss Wise / collects pins / in her leisure time.

2. "It is a disappointment / when I do not get / the pin I want," / Miss Wise said / with a chortle.

3. Perseverance is / the solution.

4. Bring a collection / of your favorite things / to class.

5. Tim wears six / of his nine hats.

6. Mike rides off / on his bike / to see Jill's collection.

7. Mike thinks Linda / should compromise / with her neighbors / and collect cats / instead of pigs.

8. Mike was uneasy / about his smile collection.

Click!

Read the sentences below. Circle words with the short *i* vowel sound. Draw a line under words with the long *i* vowel sound. Then follow the directions.

1. Jill and Lin take bikes to the lake. Add Lin's bike to the bike rack.
2. Make a swan that glides on the lake.
3. Lin takes his kite to the lake. Make a line from Lin's hand to the kite.
4. Jill wants to go for a hike. Add a hill in the back for Jill to hike up.
5. Mike skates fast. Make a smile on Mike's face.
6. Make five stripes for Mike's skates.
7. The friends will have a picnic. Make a grill for the picnic.

Name _____

Click!

Complete the story map below to summarize the selection.
Be sure to write the events in correct order.

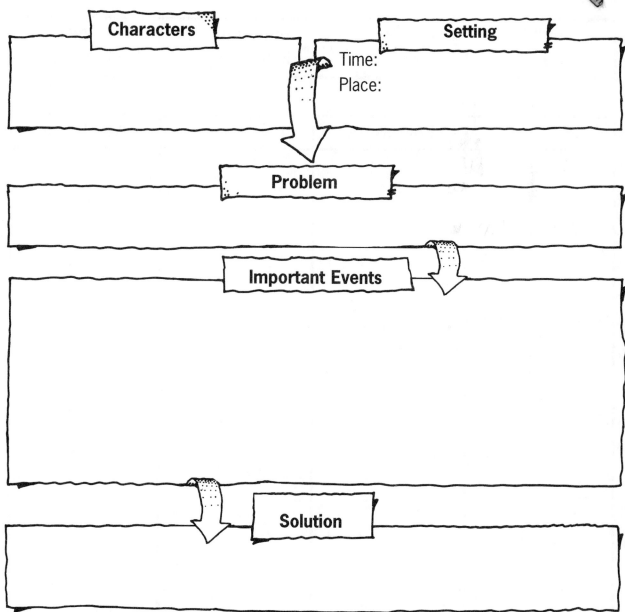

Characters

Setting

Time:
Place:

Problem

Important Events

Solution

Now use the information above to write a one-sentence summary of the story.

_____

_____

Harcourt

Prefixes, Suffixes, and Root Words

Read the following words and identify the prefixes, suffixes, and root words.

| graceful | preheat | redesign | nonfiction |
| tenderness | bicycle | improper | uninteresting |

Prefixes	Root Words	Suffixes	New Words

Harcourt

Fluency Builder

pageant	class	role
restless	able	fox
tropical	wait	hopes
rehearsals	give	jokes
attentively	nose	nose
troublesome	begin	cope
		flops
		frog

1. Miss Jones's class is planning / a holiday pageant.

2. The pageant is / about a fox, / a dog, / and a frog that visit / a tropical land.

3. Ron hopes / to get the role / of the fox / because it has / the greatest jokes.

4. During dress rehearsals, / Miss Jones gives out the costumes.

5. Everyone waits attentively / to receive his or her costume.

6. Ron's costume / is a troublesome fake fox nose / that flops up and down.

7. Everyone is restless / waiting for the pageant / to begin.

8. Ron is able to cope / with his fake fox nose.

A Troublesome Nose

Write the word that makes the sentence tell about the picture.

1. Robin has a job at Tom's map

_____ .

    hop   **pond**   **shop**

2. At the shop, they have maps and

_____ .

    groves   **globes**   **bones**

3. Tom asks Robin to

_____ the shop.

    mope   **pop**   **mop**

4. The _____

    pole   **mole**   **smoke**

of the mop hits a clock.

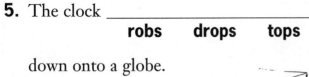

5. The clock _____

    robs   **drops**   **tops**

down onto a globe.

6. That's how Robin

_____

    rode   **hop**   **broke**

the clock and the globe.

Harcourt

A Troublesome Nose

Fill in the story map to tell about the main events in "A Troublesome Nose."
Use the words in the gray boxes to help you.

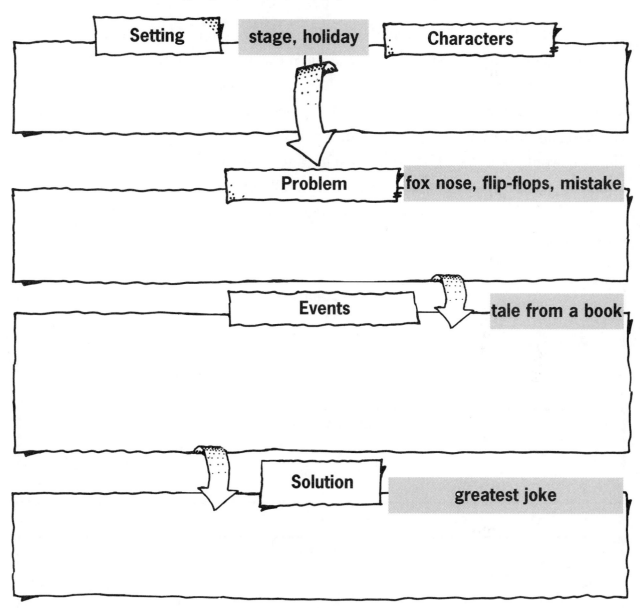

Use the information in the story map to write a one-sentence summary of
"A Troublesome Nose."

_____

_____

Narrative Elements

Read the paragraph and identify the problem, the problem-solving steps, and the resolution in the story.

Daniel walked slowly around the exhibit at the museum. He had never seen a dinosaur skeleton before. Signs all around the museum said Do Not Touch! Daniel knew better than to touch these precious bones. All of a sudden the dinosaur started to move. Daniel turned around and saw that a sleeve of the coat he had tied around his waist was now caught on the dinosaur's tail. He tried to unhook his coat, but the dinosaur wouldn't let go! The dinosaur started to sway even more. Daniel decided to untie the jacket from around his waist. He carefully untied his jacket and left it hanging from the dinosaur's tail. A security guard came by and got Daniel's jacket for him.

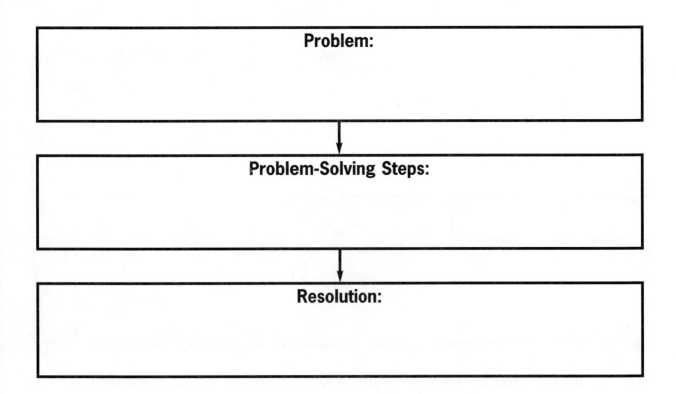

Problem:

Problem-Solving Steps:

Resolution:

Harcourt

Fluency Builder

courageous	were	agreed
immigrants	played	team
salary	first	see
tremendous	called	speed
appreciation	find	Yankees
valuable	glad	forget
modest		
sportsmanship		

1. Joe DiMaggio's parents / were immigrants.

2. He played baseball / with a team called / the Yankees.

3. At first / the fans / did not like him, / but Joe / could hit well, / and he had speed.

4. The fans then agreed / that he was a tremendous find.

5. Joe / was valuable / to the team, / and his salary / went up.

6. Baseball fans / will not forget / the courageous sportsmanship / of Joe DiMaggio.

7. He was a modest man, / but he was always glad / to see his fans.

8. He was / voted into / the Baseball Hall of Fame / in appreciation / of all that he gave / to the game.

Joe DiMaggio, One of Baseball's Greatest

Fred has a home next to the sea. A seal named Honey comes to see him. Fred feeds Honey a meal of fish. Honey eats. Then Honey dives in and out of some seaweed.

Honey swims down deep to the seabed. Honey sees a net. Honey eats a hole in the net. The fish swim free. Then Honey leaps out of the sea. Fred's feet get wet.

Circle and write the word that best completes each sentence.

1. Fred's home is _____ to the sea.   **next   bent   neat**

2. Fred meets a _____
   named Honey.   **seen   seal   meal**

3. Honey likes to _____ fish.   **eat   sweep   heat**

4. She dives to the _____.   **seabed   treetop   clean**

5. She sees a _____.   **heat   net   beam**

6. She _____ some trapped fish.   **frees   seats   seeds**

7. Then she _____ out of the sea.   **gleams   weeds   leaps**

8. Fred gets _____.   **ten   wet   wheat**

Harcourt

Joe DiMaggio, One of Baseball's Greatest

These events are from "Joe DiMaggio, One of Baseball's Greatest." They are out of order. Put a number in front of each one to show the right order.

_____ DiMaggio hit 46 home runs.

_____ DiMaggio retired.

_____ DiMaggio made the New York Yankees team.

_____ DiMaggio did not miss getting a hit in 56 games.

Now write each event from above where it belongs in the story.

_____

In 1936 he got 206 hits, and 29 of them were home runs.

His salary went up at the end of the year.

_____

In 1938 and 1939 he had many hits, but his hitting fell off a little in 1940.

_____

_____

In 1955 he was voted into the Baseball Hall of Fame.

He was 84 when his life ended on March 8, 1999.

Harcourt

Prefixes, Suffixes, and Roots

Prefix	Suffix	Root	Meaning
re-			again, back
dis-			not, opposite of
	-less		without
	-ian		person who does
	-ible		able to
		-vis-	see

Write the word that matches each definition. Choose from the words in the box below.

dishonest	**visible**	**dislikes**	**tasteless**	**weightless**
reuse	**redo**	**replace**	**musician**	**politician**

1. person who performs music _____

2. does not like _____

3. without weight _____

4. not honest _____

5. use again _____

6. person in politics _____

7. put back _____

8. able to be seen _____

9. without taste _____

10. do again _____

Harcourt

Fluency Builder

outspoken   quiet   June

practical   asked   fun

brisk   liked   tugged

elegant   with   stuff

elevations   how   stuck

miniatures   what

starstruck   day

marveled

1. Amelia said / it was a starstruck night / outside.

2. Amelia / was outspoken, / but June / was quiet.

3. Amelia liked practical pants, / but June enjoyed elegant dresses.

4. June had fun / with her miniature / tea set.

5. It was / a brisk day / and the fresh breeze / gave her an idea.

6. June marveled / at how brave / Amelia was.

7. Amelia gave June a tape / and asked / "What is / the elevation / of this shed?"

8. She tugged a box / and other stuff / out of the shed.

Amelia's Flying Lesson

Circle and write the word that answers each riddle.

1. I have the same vowel sound as in *run*.
My mom and dad are dogs. What am I?

_____

bug   tube   pup

2. I have the same vowel sound as in *rude*.
You can make a tune with me. What am I?

_____

flute   prune   trumpet

3. I have the same vowel sound as in *rut*.
I rise and set. What am I?

_____

sun   tube   tub

4. I have the same vowel sound as in *brute*.
I am made of sand. What am I?

_____

prune   mud   dune

5. I have the same vowel sound as in *hum*.
You get clean in me. What am I?

_____

rut   tub   lube

6. I have the same vowel sound as in *lute*.
I tell people what to do. What am I?

_____

stub   pollute   rule

7. I have the same vowel sound as in *bug*.
I can be filled with milk. What am I?

_____

cub   cup   glue

8. I have the same vowel sound as in *tune*.
I name a time. What am I?

_____

Jules   Jean   June

9. I have the same vowel sound as in *bud*.
You can sweep me up. What am I?

_____

stunt   dust   plume

Harcourt

Amelia's Flying Lesson

Complete the flowchart with words from the box to tell what happened in "Amelia's Flying Lesson."

climbed	flew	girls
turn	sky	wheels

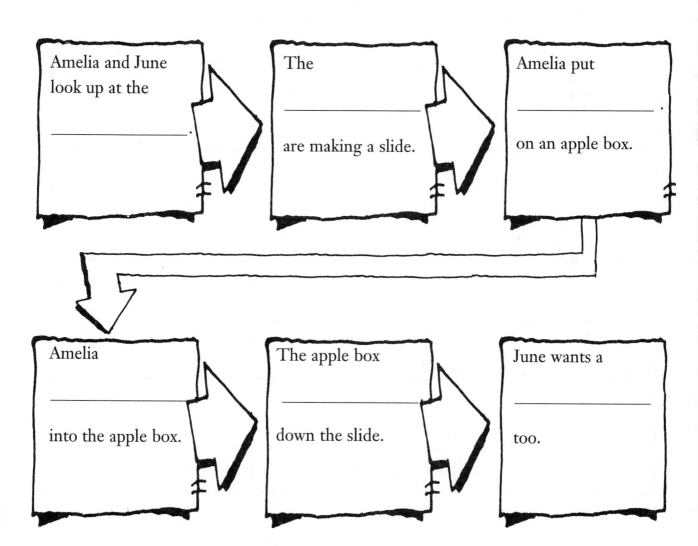

Amelia and June look up at the _____.

The _____ are making a slide.

Amelia put _____ on an apple box.

Amelia _____ into the apple box.

The apple box _____ down the slide.

June wants a _____ too.

Now write a one-sentence summary of the story. You may use the flowchart above to help you.

_____

Harcourt

Locate Information

Read the words in the box. Write them in the correct places in the first column. In the third column, tell in which part of a book each is located.

index	table of contents
preface glossary	title page

Book Part	Description	Location in Book
	includes name of book, author, publisher	
	an alphabetical list of topics with page numbers where they can be found	
	a brief introduction to a book	
	a dictionary of terms used in the book	
	a list of chapters with the page number where each can be found	

Harcourt

Fluency Builder

ad lib   began   stall
shiftless   was   Walt
luxury   song   call
privilege   that   all
elated   ask   calmly
shamefacedly   for   already
indignantly
assent

1. The CD Man / indignantly said / his business was honest.

2. Walt shamefacedly said / all he had / was five bucks.

3. Walt is not / a shiftless kid; / he is honest.

4. CDs are a luxury, / and you already / have lots / of them.

5. Walt began / to ad lib a song / outside the CD stall.

6. Walt was elated / that the CD Man asked / for the privilege / of selling his songs.

7. Walt calmly nodded his assent / and said he'd bring the songs / next week.

8. "I'd call you / a real can-do kid!" / said the CD Man.

Can-Do Kid

Read the story. Then read each question that follows the story. Circle the letter for the best answer.

It was late in the fall. Jan called Walt. She asked him to go to a baseball game with her. Walt hoped to see a ball hit over a wall. Jan and Walt met on the sidewalk close to the mall. They got on a bus. The bus went to a lot covered with grass that had white lines on it. The baseball game was at the lot.

It was time for the Rams to bat. A tall man walked to the plate with his bat. A small man who played for the Flames tossed him the ball. The batter hit the ball. The ball went over a wall. The Rams got a run. "What a fine hit!" Walt said.

1 Whom did Jan ask to go to the baseball game with her?
   A Walt
   B her dad
   C a tall man on the Rams team

2 When did they go to the game?
   A in the spring
   B in June
   C in the fall

3 What did Walt hope to see?
   A a ball at the mall
   B a ball hit over a wall
   C a small man hit a ball

4 Jan and Walt met _____.
   A in the hall
   B close to the mall
   C at the falls

5 The _____ game was at the lot.
   A ball
   B talk
   C mall

6 With a bat in hand, _____ came to the plate.
   A a bald man
   B Walt
   C a tall man

7 _____ tossed the ball to the plate.
   A A basketball
   B Walt
   C A small man

8 The man on the Rams team hit the ball over a _____.
   A wall
   B mall
   C stall

Can-Do Kid

Complete the flowchart with words from the box to tell about "Can-Do Kid."

singing	money	can-do
business	earn	stall

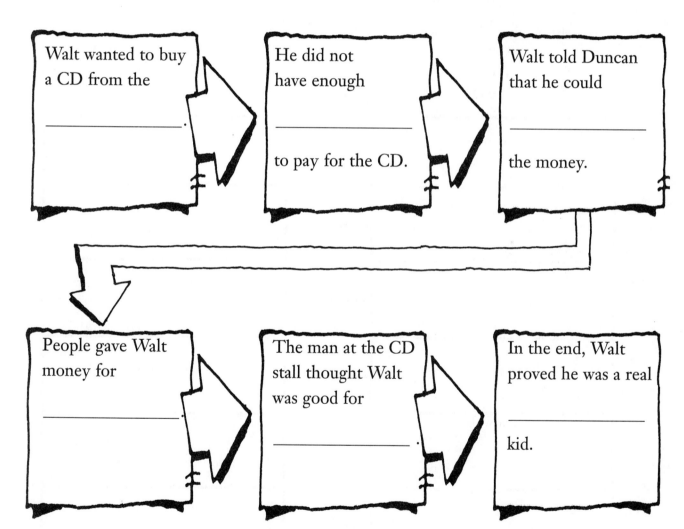

Walt wanted to buy a CD from the

_____.

He did not have enough

_____

to pay for the CD.

Walt told Duncan that he could

_____

the money.

People gave Walt money for

_____.

The man at the CD stall thought Walt was good for

_____.

In the end, Walt proved he was a real

_____

kid.

Now use the flowchart to write a one-sentence summary of the story.

_____

_____

Cause and Effect

Read each sentence. Identify the cause and the effect. Then fill in the boxes.

1. We ate lunch inside because it began to rain.
2. The car ran out of gas, so we had to walk home.
3. We forgot to add a stamp to the envelope, and our letter was returned.
4. My dad fenced in our garden because rabbits were eating the plants.
5. The sun was very hot, and our ice cream melted.
6. I brought my lunch because I didn't like the food that was being served.

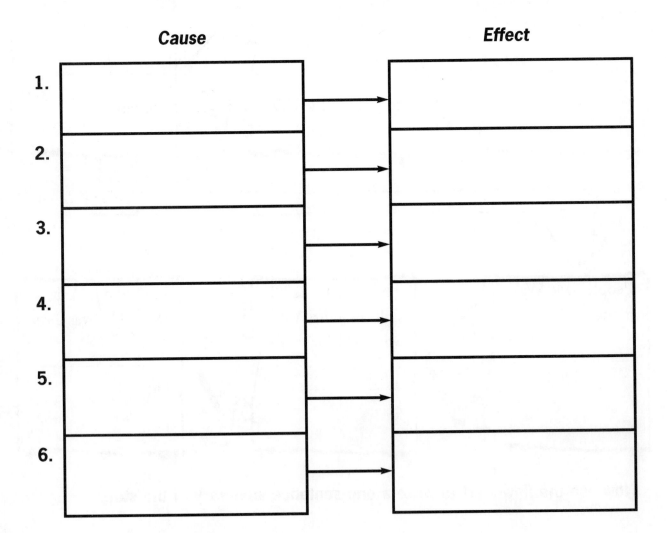

Cause   Effect

1.
2.
3.
4.
5.
6.

Harcourt

Fluency Builder

insignificant	**out**	**gray**
plotting	**rope**	**began**
twined	**sign**	**sailed**
steely	**off**	**ran**
encircling	**down**	**raiding**
loyal	**hens**	**last**
neglected		
unyielding		

1. Ray's dog, / Loyal, had / a heavy gray blanket / to sleep on.

2. Ray twined a rope / with a sign on it / to the gate.

3. Loyal stretched out / on his blanket / and began plotting / how to prove he was brave.

4. Ray neglected to close the gate, / so Loyal sailed out / and was off down the street.

5. A big dog said / that Loyal / was small and insignificant.

6. Loyal trotted / around the pen encircling the hens, / to stop the fox / from raiding the pen.

7. The fox grabbed / Loyal's leg / in his steely grip.

8. Loyal was unyielding, / and at last the fox / ran away.

Name _____

Small But Brave

Circle and write the word that makes the sentence tell about the picture.

1. Gail likes to _____ on the trail.

   tray   tramp   paid

2. Champ likes to _____ rabbits.

   chase   say   plant

3. "I think the _____ goes this way."

   trade   trail   flag

4. Gail thinks it will _____ .

   same   pain   rain

5. "My feet are wet, and so are my _____ ."

   hats   clay   braids

6. They run all the _____ back to camp.

   damp   way   stay

7. Next time, Gail will bring a _____ .

   hat   pat   ramp

Harcourt

Name _____

Small But Brave

Fill in the story map to tell about the main events in "Small But Brave." Use the words in the gray boxes to help you.

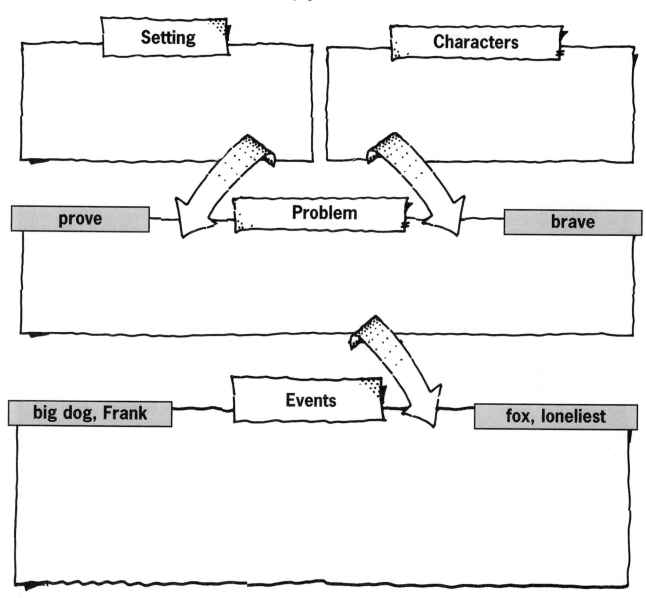

Setting

Characters

prove

Problem

brave

big dog, Frank

Events

fox, loneliest

Now use the information above to write a one-sentence summary to explain the lesson that Loyal learned.

_____

_____

Harcourt

Narrative Elements

Read the paragraph and identify the narrative elements in the story. Then fill in the story map.

One day Sarah went to the garage for her bike—but it was not there! Where could it be? She ran to ask her mother for help. Her mother suggested that she think about all the things she had done since yesterday. Sarah remembered riding to the park and leaving her bike near a tree. Then she remembered walking home with her best friend Lisa. That was it! She ran to the park, and sure enough, her bike was exactly where she had left it!

Characters	Setting

Plot

Problem

Important Events

Solution

Harcourt

Fluency Builder

uninhabited	come	chicks
burrows	started	rushed
venture	right	fresh
stranded	wanted	fishing
instinctively	years	splashed
nestle	three	with
	again	watches

1. The team / wanted to bring / the puffins back / to the uninhabited / Egg Rock.

2. The team / started with a plan / to bring / the puffins back.

3. A village / of burrows / was made / for the chicks / to nestle in.

4. The team hoped / the puffins / would instinctively return again / in two or three years.

5. The child / watches the puffin / fishing for fresh fish.

6. The children / rushed to help / the young birds that were stranded / in the village.

7. The young birds / splashed into / the water / but did not venture / out any further.

8. Steve Kress / made / the right decision / to come / to Egg Rock.

Bringing Back the Puffins

Read the sentences, and circle the words that have the /sh/, /ch/, or /th/ sound. Then follow the directions.

1. Chen, Seth, and Sasha are having lunch on a ship. Make a dish with chicken for the children.
2. They want some cheese, too. Put a big cheese next to the chicken.
3. Ships have names. Put the name "Marsha" on the side of the ship.
4. The deck of the ship will need to be cleaned. Put a big brush on the deck.
5. Seth sees a shark splashing in the sea. Put a shark in the sea.
6. Chen has a starfish that was on the beach. Put a starfish on the ship's deck.
7. There is a small shed on the deck to put things in. Make a shed on the deck.
8. Sasha will want to fish after lunch. Put a fishing pole next to the shed.
9. Seth made a batch of lemonade. Give each friend a matching glass.

Name _____

Bringing Back the Puffins

These events from "Bringing Back the Puffins" are in the wrong order. Put a number in front of each one to show the correct order.

_____ The chicks left their nests and headed for the sea.

_____ Kress and his team went to a land where puffins lived.

_____ They set up a village of nests for the puffin chicks.

_____ Steve Kress made a plan to bring puffin chicks to Egg Rock.

Now write each event in the order in which it happens in the selection. Put each one next to an X.

X _____

X _____

They brought puffin chicks back to Egg Rock.

X _____

The team fed the chicks and kept them safe from danger.

X _____

Steve Kress watched for the puffins to return to their nests.

Write a one-sentence summary to tell how the story ends.

_____

_____

Summarize

Fill out the first two columns of the K-W-L chart at the bottom of this page. In column 1, write what you know about growing vegetables. In column 2, write what you would like to learn about growing vegetables.

Now read the following paragraph about vegetable gardens.

Growing a vegetable garden requires a great deal of time and energy. In the early spring, the soil must be turned with a shovel or garden hoe. Fertilizer should be added to create a good place for your vegetables to take root. Seeds can be planted as soon as the weather turns warm. Once the seedlings begin to grow, weeds must be pulled out each week and the garden watered often. By late summer, the full-grown vegetables should be picked each day. The garden needs to be cleaned of dead plants in the fall. Delicious vegetables will be the result of all your hard work!

Complete the last column of the chart by summarizing the information you learned from the paragraph.

What I Know	What I Want to Know	What I Learned

Harcourt

Fluency Builder

haze	bike	carp
inhale	feed	garden
mural	like	harvest
lavender	smell	Marlene
skidded	big	part
	seat	Carla
	from	yard
	wanted	

1. Martin skidded his bike / to a stop, / making a haze of dust.

2. Martin wanted / to feed the carp / in the pond.

3. Miss Marlene likes to inhale / the sweet smells / from the garden / while sitting on the garden seat.

4. Nick measured neat lines / for the next part / of his garden mural.

5. The small green tomatoes were / for the next big harvest.

6. Nick saw a line of lavender petals / leaving the garden.

7. The petals led Nick / to Carla and Lil's yard.

8. Carla did her part / to show Nick / that the green tomatoes / were not useless.

Green Tomatoes

Read the story. Circle all the words with the /är/ sound you hear in *hard*.

Marta and Bart collect marbles. They like the game of marbles a lot. "We could start a marble game in the corner of the yard," says Marta. She and Bart find a spot by the barn. They make a target for the marbles in the dust.

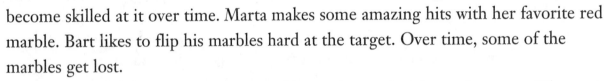

It's hard to hit a target with a marble. Marta and Bart become skilled at it over time. Marta makes some amazing hits with her favorite red marble. Bart likes to flip his marbles hard at the target. Over time, some of the marbles get lost.

Bart and Marta get the greatest marbles at the market down the street. The marbles are in a corner of the market. The friends see beans, peas, and parsnips. Then they see yarn, car wax, and a yardstick. At last they find the marbles next to the greeting cards.

Now write the word with the /är/ sound that best completes each sentence.

1. Marta and _____ collect marbles, and they like marble games.

2. They take their marbles to the corner of the _____.

3. They make a _____ by the barn.

4. Bart flips his marbles _____ at the target.

5. Marta and Bart get their marbles at the _____.

6. They find the marbles next to the greeting _____.

Green Tomatoes

Complete the sentences with a word from the box.

petals	season	garden	tomatoes	vines	measured

1. Nick's _____ is the greatest
   one on the block.

2. This _____, Nick
   sells lots of things from his garden.

3. One afternoon, Nick trimmed the

   _____ that cling to

   the walls.

4. He _____ lines
   on the wall for his garden art.

5. Then Nick sees that some of his

   _____ are missing.

6. Nick finds some _____
   and decides to find out where they lead.

Now write two or three sentences to summarize what happens in the rest of the story.

_____

_____

_____

_____

Cause and Effect

Read each pair of statements. For each pair, decide which statement is the cause and which is the effect.

There was broken glass everywhere.	The glass bottle fell on the floor.
The thunderstorm was beginning.	Our field trip was cancelled.
The back door was left open.	The cat ran outside.
The baby began to cry.	Alex made a loud noise.

Write each statement in the correct box on the chart.

Cause   **Effect**

	→	
	→	
	→	
	→	

Fluency Builder

smuggled facial displeasure endangered coordination jealous

hear some away takes through been overgrown noise

approach coax grown show own roaming

1. Did you hear / that noise? / Roaming / through the trees / is a baby orangutan!

2. A jealous orangutan / uses facial expressions / to show / its displeasure.

3. Do not / approach / a baby orangutan / or try to coax it away / from its mother.

4. The orangutan / is an / endangered animal.

5. Some / have been smuggled / out of the country.

6. It takes a lot / of coordination / to swing / through the overgrown trees.

7. When an orangutan has grown, / it makes / its own nest.

8. The poster / shows a baby orangutan / hugging its mother.

A Day with the Orangutans

Read the story. Circle all the words that have the long vowel sound of _o_.

Joan has a white goat named Snow. She takes Snow to show at the fair. Sometimes Joan has to coax Snow to get her to follow.

Snow is getting a bath. She will be clean for the show. Joan soaks her goat in a tub. She has yellow soap to make Snow's coat shine.

The next day, Snow throws up her heels at the show. Joan moans.

Snow wins a medal for the whitest coat. Owning a goat is fun but hard!

Circle and write the word that best completes each sentence.

1. Joan's _____ is named Snow.   **goat   dog   crow**

2. She takes Snow to a _____.   **shop   show   toad**

3. Joan _____ Snow in the tub.   **mows   socks   soaks**

4. The _____ soap makes Snow's coat shine.   **toast   white   yellow**

5. Snow _____ up her heels.   **throbs   goals   throws**

6. This makes Joan _____.   **grow   moan   man**

7. _____ a goat is fun.   **Bowling   Getting   Owning**

A Day with the Orangutans

Complete the flowchart with words from the box to tell what happened in "A Day with the Orangutans."

baby	expressions	practice	orphans	behavior	depend	human

You go deep into the rain forest of Borneo.

A _____ orangutan peeks at you from up in a tree.

When its mom arrives, you know the small orangutan is not one of the

_____ of the rain forest.

Just as _____ children do, this small orangutan stays close to its mom. Baby orangutans

_____ on their moms.

The orangutan mom has to deal with bad

_____ from her baby. The baby's

_____ show its feelings.

The small orangutan must

_____ a lot of skills in order to survive.

Now use the information from the flowchart to write a one-sentence summary of the selection.

_____

_____

Summarize

Read the following paragraph, and identify the important information.

Maps show many things about the world we live in. A map is a drawing of a place as you would see it from above. There can be maps of your city, your state, your country, or even your classroom. Symbols are used to represent different things on a map, such as roads, rivers, and mountains. Most maps have a key, or legend, that explains what each of the symbols means. It is important to read the key so you will be able to use your map correctly.

The Most Important Idea	Important Information That Supports the Main Idea	Information That Is Not as Important

Think about what information you would include in a summary of the paragraph. Which of the three boxes would you not include in a summary? Explain why.

_____

_____

_____

Harcourt

Fluency Builder

windbreak	**family**	**porch**
rustle	**his**	**more**
alarmed	**down**	**portrait**
paddock	**father**	**roared**
conch	**sea**	**worn**
almost	**in**	**scorched**
fire		**course**

1. Father was alarmed / when he heard / the grass rustle / in the wind.

2. His family / had almost / lost their home / in a grass fire / last summer.

3. From the porch of his house, / he can see the horses / in the paddock.

4. He pictured / how the flames / had roared loudly / as they scorched the roof.

5. Everyone / was worn out / as they put / more and more water / on the fire.

6. His son / had held onto the conch shell / that came / from their old home by the sea.

7. Of course, / Father knows / that the windbreak / now planted around the house / will slow / a fire down.

8. He feels safe / as he looks / at the family portrait / hanging / on the wall.

Name _____

A Home on the Oregon Trail

Write the word that answers each riddle. Each answer contains the same sound as the <u>or</u> in <u>for</u>, but it may be spelled differently.

1. My *or* sound is spelled *our*.
I am a number. What am I?

_____

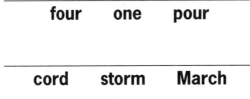

four   one   pour

2. My *or* sound is spelled *or*.
I bring wind and rain. What am I?

_____

cord   storm   March

3. Our *or* sound is spelled *oar*.
We are flat and made from trees.
What are we?

_____

boards   planks   hoards

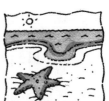

4. My *or* sound is spelled *ore*.
I am between the land
and the sea. What am I?

_____

beach   store   shore

5. My *or* sound is spelled *oor*.
You walk on me. What am I?

_____

poor   floor   grass

6. My *or* sound is spelled *or*.
You can eat me when I am
soft and white. What am I?

_____

popcorn   cord   banana

7. My *or* sound is spelled *our*.
I am part of a plant. I grow
on a vine. What am I?

_____

leaf   gourd   mourn

8. My *or* sound is spelled *or*.
If you're not careful, I can
stick you. What am I?

_____

corn   thorn   pin

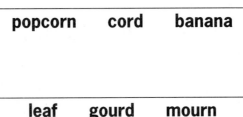

9. My *or* sound is spelled *oar*.
I am a male pig. What other
name do I have?

_____

roar   hog   boar

Harcourt

A Home on the Oregon Trail

Complete the sequence chart about "A Home on the Oregon Trail." Write a sentence in each box. The first box has been completed for you.

Event 1

Kate meets Patrick Guthrey, a traveler who takes pictures.

Event 2

Event 3

Event 4

Now use the information from the boxes to write a one-sentence summary of the selection.

_____

_____

Draw Conclusions

Read the passage. Then fill in the chart to help you draw a conclusion about Hannah. Use what you know from your experiences and what the passage tells you.

Hannah watched all of the children splashing each other. Two boys were racing each other to the floating raft. They looked as if they were having fun.

"Maybe if I just take it one step at a time I can do this. Mother says that all I need to do is move my arms and kick my legs. First I will just try holding my breath when I go under. Here I go!"

Story Information	Your Experience

Conclusion

Name _____

Fluency Builder

tutor	found	worried
glumly	around	her
impose	having	LaVerne
pastimes	hold	Pearl
irritably	some	pleasure
disposition	first	
bicker	sister	
grudge		

1. Pearl looked around glumly / and worried about sharing her room / with a new stepsister.

2. "Every summer!" / Pearl said irritably to herself.

3. Pearl found no pleasure / in having a new sister, / her happy disposition changed.

4. She felt that LaVerne / was imposing on her.

5. Pearl was holding a grudge / against her new stepsister.

6. At dinner, / the girls started / to bicker.

7. "I won't be surprised / if you find you like / some of the same pastimes," / said Pearl's stepfather.

8. At school / Pearl tutors the first graders / in reading.

Sisters Forever

Read the story below. Circle the words that have the same vowel sound as in *first*.

Sherman yearned for one perfect gift on his thirteenth birthday. He wanted a surfboard. His hands were a blur as he ripped into the first gift.

"It's a shirt. Thanks," he said. The next present was fake worms. Sherman thought this was a strange gift. He looked at Kurt, Herb, and Pearl. They were smirking. The last gift was a toy dirt bike.

"This is absurd!" Sherman said.

Herb giggled. "Okay, take the burlap cloth off that present in the corner." Under the burlap, Sherman spotted a new purple surfboard!

Sherman turned to his friends. "What a perfect gift! It was worth the wait. Thanks!"

Now read each question. Mark the letter for the best answer.

1. What day was it?
   A Thursday
   B Sherman's birthday
   C the first day of October
   D the third day of September

2. What did Sherman yearn for?
   A thirteen dollars
   B to learn to ski
   C a surfboard
   D fake worms

3. What was his first present?
   A a shirt
   B a small dirt bike
   C a turtle
   D fake worms

4. What present did Sherman find under the burlap?
   A a surfboard
   B a small dirt bike
   C a bird on a perch
   D a shirt

Sisters Forever

Write one sentence in each box below to show how Pearl and LaVerne went from disliking each other to getting along.

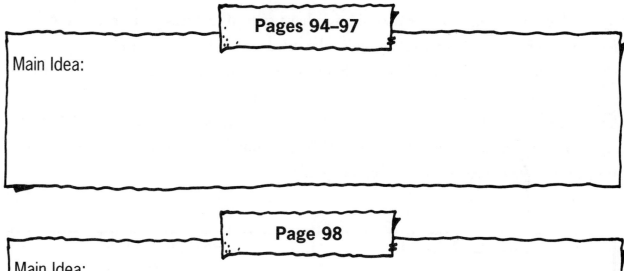

Pages 94–97

Main Idea:

Page 98

Main Idea:

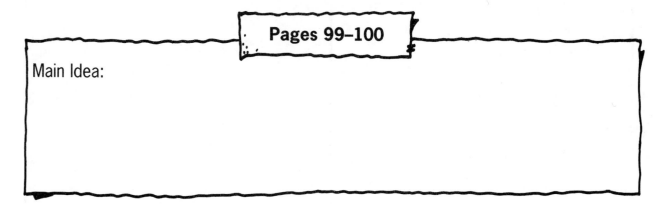

Pages 99–100

Main Idea:

Now write a one-sentence summary statement about the selection.

Compare and Contrast

Read the passage. Compare and contrast the two types of animals you read about.

Both hot- and cold-weather animals have special features that protect them from the outside. Hot-weather animals, like mice and jackrabbits, can dig underground to keep cool. They also have big ears and tails that help their bodies lose heat. Cold-weather animals, such as the polar bear, have thick coats of fur to keep them warm. These animals generally have small ears and tails. This helps them stay warm by trapping their body heat. Whether animals live where it is hot or cold, they all know how to get away from danger.

How the Animals Are Alike	How the Animals Are Different

Harcourt

Fluency Builder

acquaintance   called   Mavis
scrounging   hungry   acorns
eavesdropping   any   Iris
excitable   believe   find
wistfully   they   dry
sympathetically   sadly
logical   menu
    idea

1. Mavis, / the jay, / and her acquaintance, / Iris, / the deer, / were picking through / a pile of dry leaves.

2. "I believe / it will be a long winter," / Mavis said / sadly.

3. Bo, / the wood rat, / was eavesdropping. / He said. / "My winter menu / will be acorns, / if I can find any!"

4. "When snow covers the leaves, / it makes it hard for you to eat, / Iris," / Mavis said / sympathetically.

5. "Yes, / I find myself / scrounging for food / and thinking wistfully / about spring," / said Iris.

6. "I have a logical plan!" / called Bo.

7. "If we all / work together, / we won't go hungry."

8. The idea / made the animals excitable. / They couldn't wait / for the acorns / to fall!

Oak Grove Picnic

Read the sentences and follow the directions.

1. It is a sunny day. Add the sun to the sky.
2. Tony is in the kitchen. Put an apron on him.
3. He has water in a mug. Put zebra stripes on the mug.
4. Tony will fry some potato pancakes. Circle the potatoes.
5. He also will make a salad. Add some slices of tomato to the bowl near Tony.
6. Tony's sister will help him. Give Amy a chef's hat.
7. Amy's apron is old. Rewrite her name on the apron.
8. Amy grinds some pepper. Add pepper to the bowl below the grinder.

For each word below, write a word from above that has the same long vowel sound and a similar spelling.

acorn _____   cold _____

mind _____   sly _____

Harcourt

Oak Grove Picnic

Complete the sequence chart about "Oak Grove Picnic." Write a sentence or two in each box. The first box has been done for you.

**Event 1
(Page 102)**

Ruben, the squirrel, tells the other animals that the acorns are ripe and it's time to go to the oak grove.

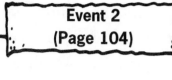

**Event 2
(Page 104)**

**Event 3
(Page 105)**

**Event 4
(Pages 106–107)**

Use the information from the boxes above to write a one-sentence summary of the story.

_____

_____

_____

Draw Conclusions

Read the passage. Then fill in the chart to help you draw a conclusion about Matt's actions.

"Easy out," shouted the kids in the outfield.

Matt watched Sam, his younger brother, step up to the plate. Matt was the best ball player around. Sam was the worst batter around. And today Matt's team was playing against Sam's. Sam looked so small standing there. Matt could hear his own teammates making fun of his brother.

Amazingly, Sam hit a pop fly. The ball headed straight for Matt. But Matt didn't raise his glove fast enough to catch the ball. As Sam reached first base, Matt gave his brother a thumbs-up. Then he just shrugged his shoulders at his angry teammates in the outfield.

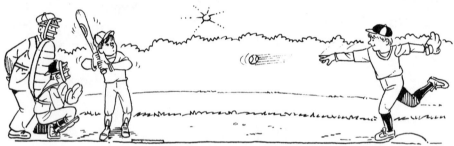

Story Information
Your Own Knowledge
Conclusion You Can Draw

Harcourt

Fluency Builder

hysterically	letter	might
overwhelm	with	frightening
interpreter	fun	sights
appetizing	think	flight
equivalent	food	tries
irrigation	many	
occasionally	bike	
	new	

1. Michelle's neighbor / is the interpreter / of Kim's letters.

2. Irrigation makes rice fields / muddy to walk in.

3. Michelle occasionally / tries to eat rice, / but having to eat it / with every meal / might overwhelm her.

4. Is a canoe / the equivalent / of a rowboat?

5. Kim had fun / seeing all / of the new sights / in Ho Chi Minh City.

6. Michelle thinks / many of the foods / in the market / sound appetizing.

7. It would be frightening / to ride a bike / next to so many cars.

8. Michelle was hysterically happy / when her mom agreed / to take a flight to Vietnam.

A Pen Pal in Vietnam

Read the story. Circle the words in which _igh_ stands for the long _i_ sound. Then draw a line under the words in which _ie_ stands for the long _i_ sound.

Last night Harry went to the fair. Two clowns wore bright helmets. Each tied a cloth to his helmet, one red and one blue. At first they pretended to fight. The red clown spilled ink on the blue clown's tights. The blue clown soaked the red clown with water from a hose. So the red clown dried himself with the blue clown's cape. Then they both got on mighty horses. Each clown carried a whipped-cream pie. When they passed each other, they tossed the pies. Then Harry cried with delight when the whipped cream splattered on the clowns. Never before had he seen such a funny sight.

After the show was over, Harry had a bright idea. A clown's job might be just right for him! He tried on some tights and applied for a job at the fair.

Now write the long _i_ word from above that best completes each sentence.

1. Each clown _____ a cloth to his helmet.

2. The blue clown's _____ had ink spilled on them.

3. The red clown _____ himself off with the blue clown's cape.

4. Both clowns rode on _____ horses.

5. Each carried a whipped-cream _____.

6. Harry had never before seen such a funny _____.

7. He thinks that being a clown _____ be fun.

A Pen Pal in Vietnam

**Write one or two sentences in each box below
to tell how Michelle's life and Kim's life are
alike and different.**

Pages 110–113

How do Kim's meals compare to the meals eaten by Michelle?

Page 114

How does the traffic in Ho Chi Minh City probably compare to the traffic in Michelle's small town?

Pages 115–116

How does the way people dress in Vietnam compare to the way people dress in the United States?

Use the information above to write a one-sentence summary about the selection.

_____

_____

Harcourt

Compare and Contrast

Read the passage. Then use the Venn diagram to compare and contrast the inventors you read about.

The Wright brothers and Robert Fulton are famous inventors. They all built machines that help people get from one place to another. On August 17, 1807, people in New York City were laughing at Fulton when his steamboat did not run at first. But the *Clermont* finally worked and made river travel important for America. Orville and Wilbur Wright looked to the sky to help people travel. On December 17, 1903, the first powered aircraft, *The Wright Flyer*, made four successful flights in Kitty Hawk, North Carolina. Although they had many failures, these inventors were also brave to keep trying.

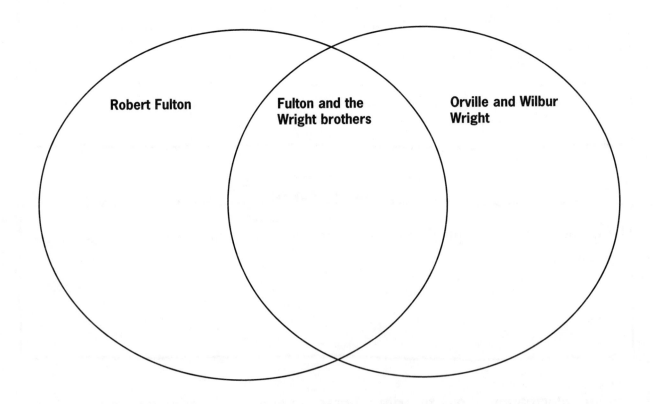

Robert Fulton

Fulton and the
Wright brothers

Orville and Wilbur
Wright

Harcourt

Fluency Builder

tundra	sometimes	howls
piteously	across	power
surrender	when	amount
cease	between	down
abundant	tails	sounds
bonding	that	mouth
	may	snout

1. A wolf howls / across the tundra.

2. If a pack member dies, / all the other wolves / howl piteously.

3. Wolves squeak / when they are bonding / with each other.

4. Sometimes wolves use their tails / to communicate.

5. A wolf may hold / another wolf's snout / in its mouth.

6. There is an abundant amount / of communication / between wolves / in a pack.

7. When another wolf / meets an alpha wolf, / it holds its tail down, / to say that it is willing / to surrender its power / to the leader.

8. The sounds / of the wolves / will not cease to be heard / across the tundra.

Wolf Pack: Sounds and Signals

Circle and write the word that makes the sentence tell about the picture.

1. Farmer May dug with her _____.

                            plow   **scowl**   **house**

2. She came upon a big hole in the _____.

                             spout   **grand**   **ground**

3. Farmer May wiped her _____.

                        prow   **brow**   **sound**

4. "Did the _____ dig this hole?"

                 sow   **clown**   **sod**

5. "Was it the _____?"

                 prowl   **pouch**   **cow**

6. At that moment, a _____ ran by.

                   frown   **mouse**   **sprout**

7. Farmer May heard a loud _____.

                        chow   **growl**   **scout**

8. "It was my _____ that made

                 town   **hound**   **hand**

the hole in the ground!" she said.

Name _____

Wolf Pack: Sounds and Signals

Write one or two sentences in each box below to show how wolves "talk" to each other.

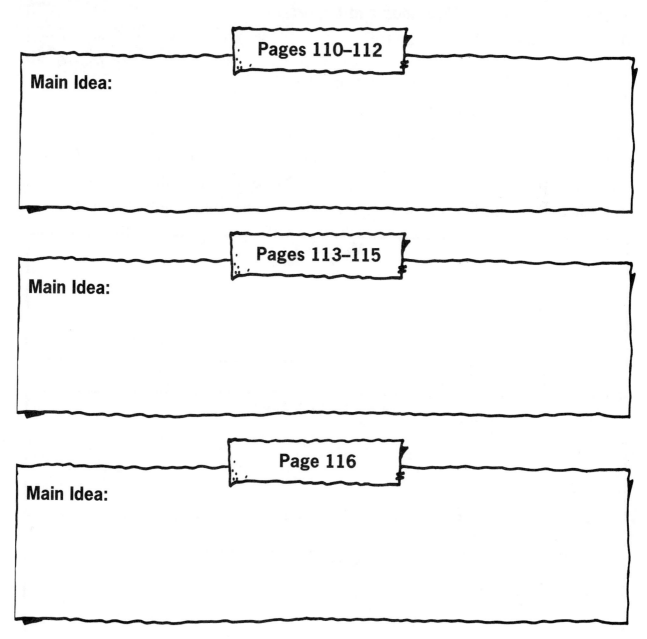

Pages 110–112

Main Idea:

Pages 113–115

Main Idea:

Page 116

Main Idea:

Write a one-sentence summary statement about the selection.

_____

_____

Summarize

Read the passage. Then fill in the boxes below. Use what you wrote in the *Main Idea* and *Important Details* boxes to write a summary.

What is black and white and travels in a herd? Why, a zebra of course! Zebras are social animals just like wolves. They travel in groups in order to stay safe. Together, they have many eyes and ears to listen for their enemies. Zebras can also talk to each other and use facial expressions to show how they feel. If a zebra gets separated from the group, the others will search for it until it is found. A herd of zebras is like a big family of animals.

Main Idea

Important Details

Summary

Fluency Builder

document	because	pencils
prosthetic	hold	device
device	their	ice
disabilities	them	space
circular	want	places
scholarship	already	
modify	new	
	idea	

1. Ernest Hamwi invented a cone / with a circular opening / to hold ice cream.

2. Two men invented pencils / with erasers / on the end of them.

3. The shopping cart / was invented / because shoppers needed / more space in their baskets.

4. Puzzles were invented / to help children / learn about places / around the world.

5. You may want to modify / an invention / that is already in use.

6. A new prosthetic device / can help people / with disabilities.

7. A patent / is a document / that protects your idea.

8. Taking the time / to find out / how to make / your invention better / is a sign / of good scholarship.

Who Invented This?

Read the story. Circle all the words in which _c_ stands for the /s/ sound.

Cecil lives in Cedar Falls. Bruce is his cat.

His family has a home outside the city. He thinks it is a fine place.

His home has a cellar. Bruce looks for mice.

Cecil likes to race his bicycle everywhere.

He goes to the Cinema Palace, where a ticket costs just fifty cents.

Cecil likes to see films about outer space.

Circle and write the word that best completes each sentence.

1. Cecil's cat is named _____ .   **Brenda**   **Bruce**   **Brute**

2. Cecil lives near the _____ .   **circus**   **city**   **pace**

3. His home has a _____ .   **corridor**   **spice**   **cellar**

4. He rides his _____ everywhere.   **cyclops**   **bicycle**   **cyclist**

5. At the Cinema Palace, tickets cost just fifty _____ .

   cents   **peace**   **cans**

6. He likes movies about outer _____ best.

   space   **fence**   **specks**

Who Invented This?

In each box below, name the invention and describe what it does.

Page 126

Invention:

What It Does:

Page 127

Invention:

What It Does:

Page 128

Invention:

What It Does:

Page 129

Invention:

What It Does:

Page 130

Invention:

What It Does:

Write a one-sentence summary about the selection.

_____

_____

Main Idea and Details

Read the following paragraph as you think about which sentence states the main idea, or what the paragraph is mainly about. Then fill in the chart. Each detail should be one idea from the paragraph.

Our School Playground

Our school playground is a great place to play. It has a climbing tower to hang from. It has long, short, and tunnel slides. It even has a rope bridge! My favorite place on the playground is the fire pole because I can slide down it faster than anyone I know!

Main Idea	
Detail	**Detail**
Detail	**Detail**

Fluency Builder

muttered	see	fudge
strengthening	come	village
sculptor	work	gentle
straightaway	find	giant
retorted	talk	large
alibi	found	Gina
	they	Angela

1. Gina Ginetti is a well-known / girl detective.

2. All of the citizens had come / to the village square / to see the work / of a local sculptor revealed.

3. The Gentle Giant is / Fudge Corners's best-known dog.

4. "I don't see / what all the fuss is about," / Al muttered.

5. "Let's find Reggie / and talk to him / straightaway," / said Gina.

6. Al found / the support of Gina / and Angela strengthening / and they searched the large crowd.

7. "I have an alibi / for last night," / Reggie retorted.

8. How did Gina know / that Reggie had stolen / Al's statue?

Name _____

The Case of the Strange Sculptor

Write the word that answers each riddle.

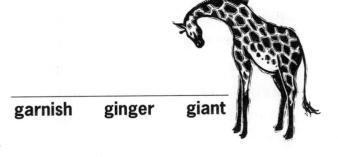

1. I begin like *giraffe*. I make things taste good. What am I?

_____

garnish　　ginger　　giant

2. I begin like *gentle*. You can play basketball inside me. What am I?

_____

gym　　garage　　gem

3. I begin like *general*. I am very, very smart. What am I?

_____

grown-up　　gem　　genius

4. I have the same *g* sound as in *original*. I help cars go. What am I?

_____

page　　gas　　engine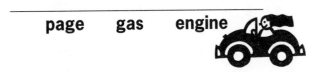

5. I end like *judge*. I can help you cross a river. What am I?

_____

nudge　　bridge　　wagon

6. I have the sound that the letter *g* stands for in *clergy*. I can make you sick. What am I?

_____

germ　　sugar　　gentle

7. I end like *badge*. I am like a big bush. What am I?

_____

fidget　　hedge　　garden

8. I have the sound that the letter *g* stands for in *change*. I am someone you don't know. Who am I?

_____

stranger　　gardener　　hinge

9. I have the sound that the letter *g* stands for in *large*. I tell how old you are. What am I?

_____

energy　　gift　　age

Harcourt

The Case of the Strange Sculptor

Write one or two sentences in each box below to sum up the story. Be sure to write the events in correct order.

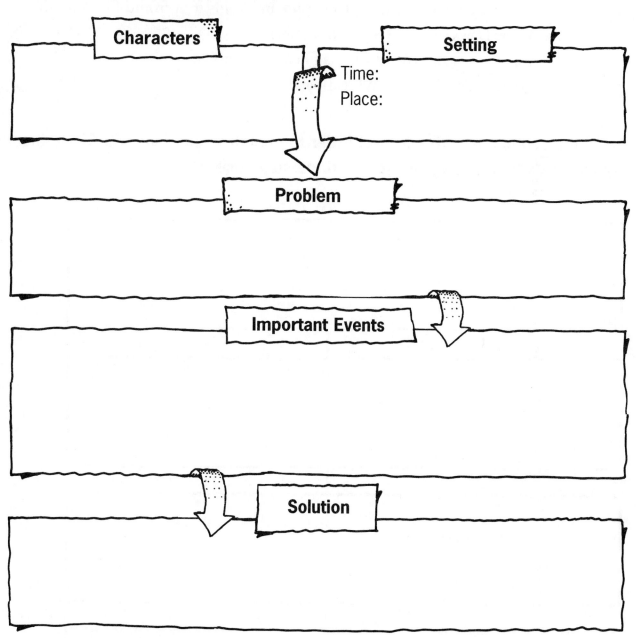

Characters

Setting

Time:
Place:

Problem

Important Events

Solution

Now use the story map to write a one-sentence summary of the story.

Name _____

Sequence

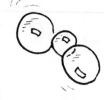

These sentences are not in the correct sequence.

Then, he removes the bubble wand and holds it in front of his mouth.

First, Luis opens the bottle of bubbles.

Finally, the air around Luis is filled with bubbles.

Next, Luis takes a deep breath and blows.

Write the sentences in the correct order to complete the diagram. Circle the signal words that help you understand the sequence.

```
┌─────────────────────────────────────────┐
│                                         │
│                                         │
│                                         │
└─────────────────────────────────────────┘
                    ↓
┌─────────────────────────────────────────┐
│                                         │
│                                         │
│                                         │
└─────────────────────────────────────────┘
                    ↓
┌─────────────────────────────────────────┐
│                                         │
│                                         │
│                                         │
└─────────────────────────────────────────┘
                    ↓
┌─────────────────────────────────────────┐
│                                         │
│                                         │
│                                         │
└─────────────────────────────────────────┘
```

Harcourt

Fluency Builder

thrifty	upon	coin
generous	all	annoyed
roguish	from	oinking
rascally	when	toiled
fascinated	there	soiled
	hens	joyfully
	pigs	
	away	
	his	

1. The farmer was thrifty / and he insisted / upon saving every coin.

2. The farmer saved / a generous fortune.

3. He became fascinated / by all of his riches.

4. The farmer's rascally friend / made up a roguish plan / to stop the farmer / from boasting.

5. When the farmer toiled / in his fields / his clothes became soiled / and his face was wet.

6. When the farmer purchased / more pigs and hens, / there was a lot / of extra oinking and clucking / on his farm.

7. The farmer became annoyed / with his friend.

8. The farmer joyfully gave away / the fields, / the pigs, / and the hens / that were making him unhappy.

Just Enough Is Plenty

Mark the answer in front of the sentence that tells about the picture.

1 **A** Roy has a coil of rope.
   B Roy digs in the soil.
   C Roy has a royal hat.
   D Roy makes his choice.

2 **A** Dan eats some oysters.
   B Dan has a gold coin.
   C Dan's lunch is spoiled now.
   D Dan looks for the foil.

3 **A** Gwen is annoyed by the bee.
   B The bee destroys Gwen's snack.
   C Gwen enjoys her blocks.
   D Gwen joins a club with Roy.

4 **A** He boils broth in a pot.
   B That cloth is soiled.
   C He hears a noise in the corner.
   D He is disappointed by the rain.

5 **A** Liz points at Roy.
   B Liz uncoils the rope.
   C Liz embroiders her name.
   D Liz has a soiled hat.

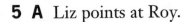

6 **A** Brinda gives a coin to the boy.
   B Brinda loiters by the exit.
   C Brinda's bike is destroyed.
   D Brinda avoids the soiled rug.

Name

Just Enough Is Plenty

Complete the story map to help you summarize the story. Be sure to write the events in the correct order.

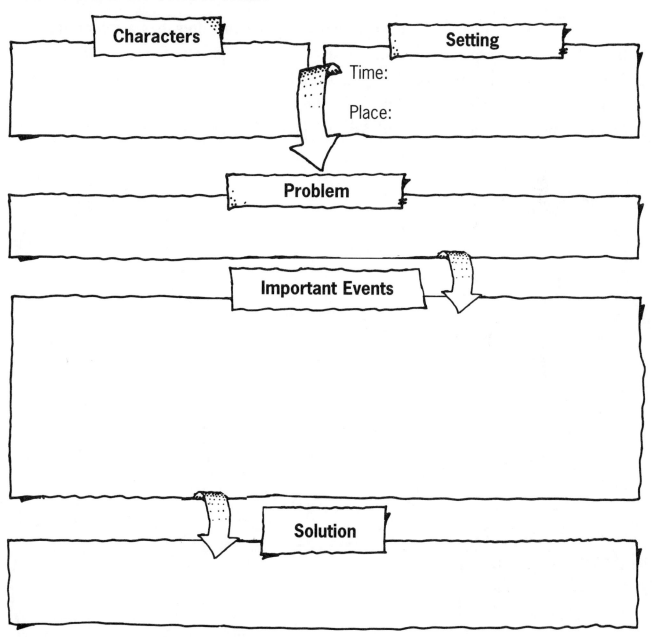

Characters

Setting

Time:

Place:

Problem

Important Events

Solution

Now write a one-sentence summary of the story.

Name _____

Main Idea and Details

Read the paragraph and identify the main idea and details. Complete the web.

Trees have many uses, both when they are living and after they are cut down. Because trees use carbon dioxide and make oxygen, they help reduce air pollution. Trees also provide habitats for birds and other animals. Both people and animals get food from many kinds of trees. After trees are cut down, we use them for many products including paper and wood. You can probably think of many other uses, too.

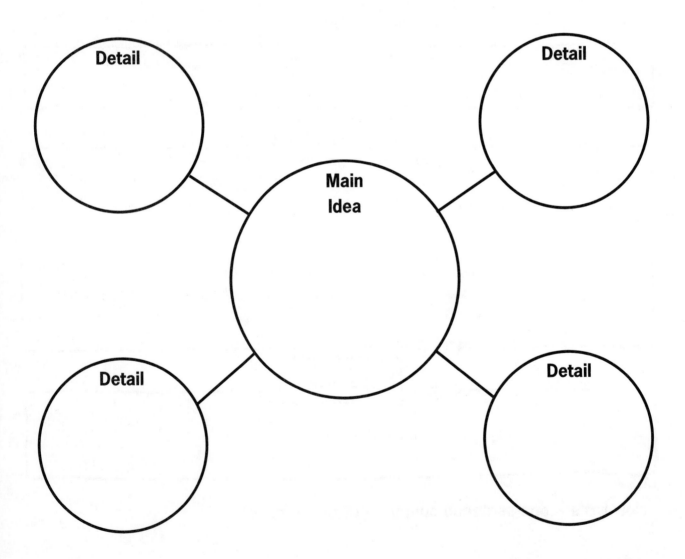

Fluency Builder

script	yell	because
triumphantly	you're	caught
desperately	that's	yawn
injustice	I've	dawn
repentant	lost	awful
acceptable		lawyer
discards		fault
circumstances		

1. Eating is usually acceptable, / unless you're the Big Bad Wolf / trying to eat a grandmother.

2. Judge Bo Peep exclaimed, / "That's awful!"

3. "I've been up since dawn," / she said with a yawn, / "and I've got lost sheep / that have to be caught."

4. The lawyer triumphantly yelled, / "You see? / He did it!"

5. The Big Bad Wolf / was not even repentant / of his crime.

6. The Big Bad Wolf cried, / "This is an injustice. / It's the author's fault / because he wrote the script."

7. The wolf desperately claimed / he was a victim of circumstances.

8. The wolf discards / the testimony / of Red Riding Cap.

Big Bad Wolf and the Law

Read the sentences and do what they tell you.

1. Dawn and Paula are having a picnic. Draw a picnic basket on the blanket.
2. Give Dawn a straw so she can drink her milk.
3. The hawk caught a garden snake. Put a small snake in the hawk's claws.
4. Draw some leaves on the lawn under the tree.
5. Don't let the dripping water go to waste! Put a bucket under the faucet.
6. The dog is bored. Draw a toy between its paws so it can play.
7. Some ants are crawling to the picnic basket. Draw a line of ants on the blanket.
8. The fawn is eating berries from the hedge. Give the fawn more berries to eat.

Now circle the words that have the vowel sound you hear in *saw* and *taught*.

Harcourt

Name _____

Big Bad Wolf and the Law

Complete the story map below to summarize the selection. Be sure to write the events in correct order.

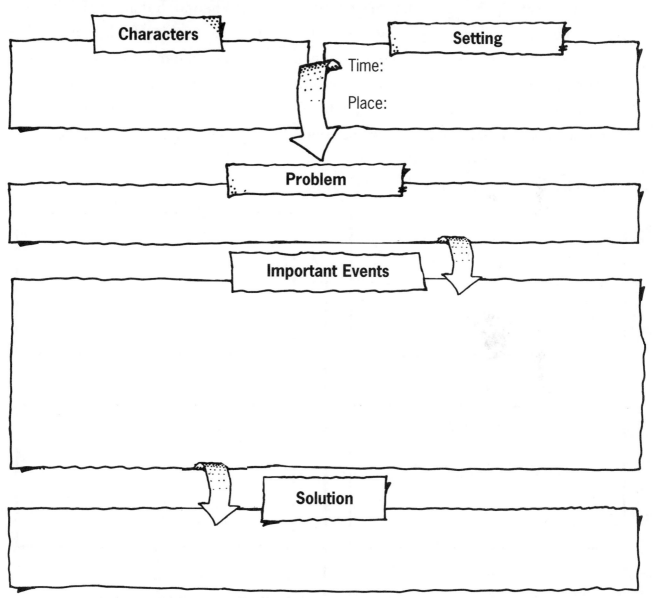

Characters

Setting

Time:

Place:

Problem

Important Events

Solution

Use the story map above to write a one-sentence summary of the story.

_____

_____

_____

Harcourt

Sequence

Read the following paragraph and identify the sequence of events.

There once was a girl who was locked up in a tower so high that it reached the clouds. The girl knew no way to escape her fate. There was nothing for her to do all day but watch her hair grow longer and longer and longer. One morning, as she was brushing her hair, she crafted a clever plan to escape. First, she tied her hair into a long braid. Next, she managed to cut the braid off with a sharp rock in the tower. Then, she tied the braid to a table in the room. Finally, she threw the rest of the braid out the window toward the ground. After she climbed down her clever rope, she ran bald-headed all throughout the town!

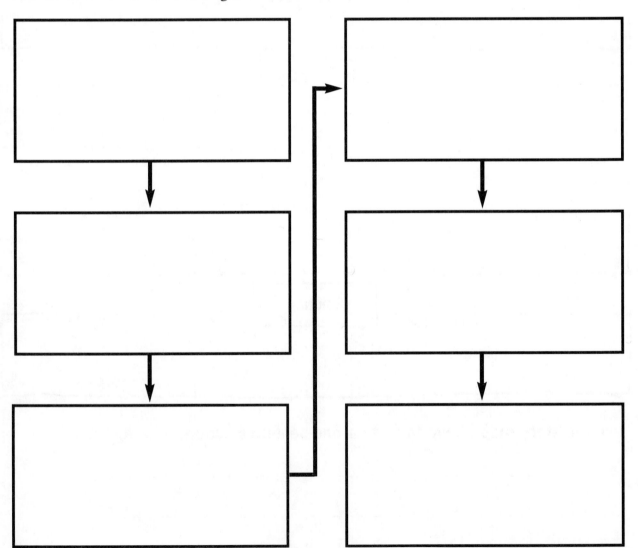

Harcourt

Fluency Builder

decreed	through	good
famine	king	Woodlandia
implored	many	firewood
trickled	old	looked
plentifully	was	books
	work	should
	down	would
		shook

1. The good kingdom / of Woodlandia / was free from famine / for many years.

2. The kingdom was also / plentifully supplied / with firewood.

3. King Roger decreed / that all of his subjects / should dress exactly like him.

4. How could they dress / like the king?

5. The Woodlandians / implored the ministers, / "Please tell us / what we should do!"

6. The ministers / looked through / rare old books / of wisdom, / hoping to find a solution.

7. Would their clever plan / work?

8. King Roger shook / with laughter / until tears trickled / down his cheeks.

A Clever Plan

Read the story. Circle the words that have the vowel sound you hear in took and would.

Woody and Eric are packing for a hike. They will cross the woods on foot. They hope to camp by a brook. Woody grabs a camping book. "Should I take this book?" he asks.

Eric looks at it. "Yes. It would tell us what to do if we got lost."

"Good thinking," Woody tells him. "What else should I take?"

"Snacks," Eric says, "and a wool jacket to keep warm."

"You are good at this," Woody tells him.

Eric says, "It gets easy with practice."

Woody's backpack is stuffed, but he wants to take two more things. "Eric, could you take the football and the extra raisins?" he asks.

Eric looks in his pack and frowns. "I have space for only one of them. What should I do?"

Woody smiles. "Leave the football," he says. "We may need the extra raisins for energy."

Eric tells him, "You know, you are good at this, too."

Now write the circled word that best completes each sentence.

1. Eric and Woody will travel on _____ across the woods.

2. They hope to camp by a _____.

3. Eric tells Woody to take the camping _____.

4. He also tells Woody to pack snacks and a _____ jacket.

5. Woody thinks Eric is _____ at deciding what to pack.

6. Eric frowns after he _____ in his pack.

7. The raisins or the _____ can fit, but not both.

8. Woody thinks they _____ leave the football.

Harcourt

Name _____

A Clever Plan

Write sentences in each box below to summarize the story. Be sure to write the events in the correct order.

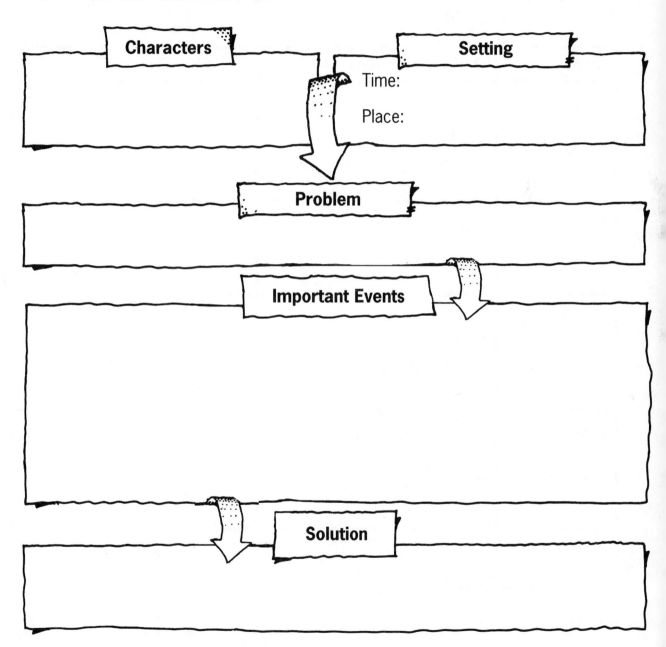

Characters

Setting

Time:

Place:

Problem

Important Events

Solution

Use the information in the boxes to write a one-sentence summary of the story.

_____

_____

Harcourt

Compare and Contrast

Think about how "One Grain of Rice" and "A Clever Plan" are alike and different. Fill in the chart. Use the chart to help you answer the questions.

Story	"One Grain of Rice"	"A Clever Plan"
Characters	Rani the raja	
Setting	long ago India	
Plot	The raja's decree causes the people of India to go hungry. Rani's cleverness saves her people.	
Lesson	Possible response: Leaders should be wise and fair.	

1. How are the settings of the stories alike? _____

2. How are the settings different? _____

_____

3. How are the plots of the stories alike? _____

_____

Harcourt

Fluency Builder

dedication	old	true
billowing	animal	renews
brigade	again	new
ventilate	very	fireproof
flammable	near	soon
curfew	after	too
	come	
	sometimes	

1. Old trees / are very flammable, / and even new shoots / are not fireproof.

2. High winds / can ventilate a fire / and send up / billowing flames.

3. When a fire / is near a camp, / rangers set a curfew.

4. New members / of a fire brigade / soon show / their dedication.

5. But / sometimes / it takes a big rainstorm / to put out a fire.

6. It is true / that fire / renews a forest.

7. After a fire, / the animals / come back.

8. Plants / grow again, / too.

Name _____

Fire in the Forest

Make the sentences tell about the pictures. Circle and write the words that have the same vowel sound as in _blue_.

1. Yesterday Drew's class went to the city

_____.

park   zoo   moon

2. First, the children went to see the new

_____ and her brood.

panda   mouse   goose

3. After eating, the baby geese

_____.

spoon   swam   snoozed

4. Then the children saw a baby

_____ and its mom.

horse   glue   moose

5. The children watched as the keeper gave

the moose some _____.

food   juice   straw

6. At _____ it was time for the

noon   room   midday

children to eat lunch, too.

7. Drew shared some _____ with his

friend Sue.   **cookies   chips   fruit**

8. Drew told Sue, "Some day I would like to be a zookeeper,

_____."

threw   too   also

Harcourt

Name _____

Fire in the Forest

Write one sentence in each box below to tell what you learned in "Fire in the Forest."

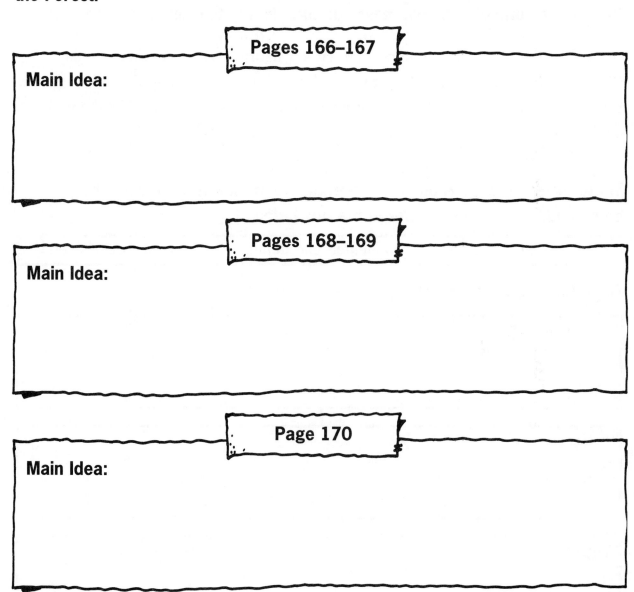

Pages 166–167

Main Idea:

Pages 168–169

Main Idea:

Page 170

Main Idea:

Use the information above to write a one-sentence summary statement about the selection.

_____

_____

Elements of Nonfiction: Text Structure

Read the following nonfiction passage and identify the text structure.

March 1, 1872, was an important day for nature lovers. That was the day President Grant signed the bill that made Yellowstone the world's first national park. In 1894 Congress passed a law that protected the park's wildlife. In 1972 the park held a big celebration for its 100th birthday. Today tourists enjoy many different activities in Yellowstone.

In what kind of text structure are events told in the order in which they happened? Circle your answer in the box below.

compare and contrast	main idea and details	sequence of events

Fill in the chart with what happened on each date.

March 1, 1872

↓

1894

↓

1972

↓

Today

Harcourt

Fluency Builder

enrich	were	from
petitioners	to	world
obliged	who	come
examiner	their	gnawed
apologized	some	know
certificate	said	written
resounded	here	

1. The hall resounded / with the noise / of the people talking.

2. Petitioners / from all over the world / were waiting / to know their future.

3. First / they were obliged / to see / an examiner.

4. The examiners / checked a written certificate / for each person.

5. A bad feeling / gnawed at the petitioners / as they waited / for a doctor.

6. They had learned / that some doctors / were forced to apologize.

7. "We regret / that you cannot stay here," / the doctors said to immigrants / who were sick.

8. Those who were allowed to come in / enriched their lives / in the United States.

Harcourt

A Place of New Beginnings

Circle and write the word that answers each riddle.

1. I have the same beginning sound as in *know*.
I am a part of your leg. What am I? _____

   kick   knee   knock

2. I have the same beginning sound as in *wrench*.
I mean the same as *incorrect*. What am I? _____

   fake   wrap   wrong

3. I have the same beginning sound as in *gnash*.
I look like a tiny fly. What am I? _____

   gnat   bee   gnaw

4. I have the same beginning sound as in *knife*.
You can untie me. What am I? _____

   knob   knot   bag

5. I have the same beginning sound as in *write*.
You can use me to tell time. What am I? _____

   wrapper   clock   wristwatch

6. I have the same ending sound as in *align*.
I tell you which way to go. What am I? _____

   sigh   singer   sign

7. I have the same beginning sound as in *knit*.
You can put books in me. What am I? _____

   knapsack   knuckle   bookbag

8. I have the same beginning sound as in *wreck*.
I am a kind of cowboy. What am I? _____

   wagon   wrangler   wrist

9. I have the same beginning sound as in *wrong*.
I am a bird. What am I? _____

   sparrow   wren   willow

Harcourt

A Place of New Beginnings

Complete the main-idea chart to tell what Karen discovers in "A Place of New Beginnings." Write a sentence in each box. The first one has been done for you.

Main Idea (page 174):

Immigrants to the United States, like Karen's great-great-grandfather, first came to Ellis Island as petitioners to enter the country.

Main Idea (pages 175–176):

Main Idea (page 179):

Main Idea (page 180):

Now use the information from the boxes to write a one-sentence summary of the selection.

_____

_____

_____

_____

Harcourt

Author's Purpose

Read the passage. Decide if the author is writing to inform, to entertain, or to persuade. Then fill in the chart with the details that helped you determine the author's purpose.

Our country is beautiful. But in many places the beauty is hidden. It is hidden by piles of litter. It is every citizen's job to keep our country free of litter. Good citizens do not litter! They throw things away in the proper places. If you want to keep our country beautiful, you should stop littering. You can even lead a monthly neighborhood cleanup. Please keep our country clean!

Author's Purpose

Details
1. Good citizens do not litter!
2.
3.

Harcourt

Fluency Builder

spiny	flower	phase
topple	find	photograph
decomposes	many	geography
brush	would	rough
habitat	you	tough
teeming	from	enough
perch		
nectar		

1. Do you think / taking photographs / in the desert / would be dull?

2. You might be surprised / to learn / that the desert's rough geography, / is teeming / with interesting life forms.

3. The desert / is a fine habitat / for plants and animals / that are tough enough / to survive there.

4. If you look closely / at a tall, spiny cactus, / you might see a tiny bird / sipping nectar / from a cactus flower.

5. Old cactuses topple / and decompose / into interesting shapes.

6. At noon / you may find animals / escaping from the heat / in the shade / of scrubby desert brush.

7. Some insects / spend a phase of their life / under the ground, / but many / can be seen in plain sight.

8. Bats perch in caves by day, / but you can photograph them / when they leave their caves / at dusk.

Name _____

Desert Animals

Read the letter. Then read each question that follows. Circle the letter of the best answer choice.

Dear Ralph,

In class today we talked about different inventions that have helped people express themselves. Before the first alphabet was invented, people wrote using pictographs, or simple drawings. Among the first written words were drawings of stars and animals.

Alfred Vail helped Samuel Morse invent the code for the telegraph. Alexander Graham Bell invented the telephone in 1876.

The phonograph was invented by Thomas Edison in 1877. A phonograph was a machine that played recorded music.

I wonder who invented laughter. It's my favorite way to express myself. When things get tough, laughing often helps me feel better.

Write back soon!

Your friend,
Phyllis

1 What did Alexander Graham Bell invent?
   A telegraph
   B television
   C roughness
   D telephone

2 Morse and Vail invented a code for the ___.
   A telephone
   B elephant
   C photograph
   D telegraph

3 Before there was an ___, people wrote using pictographs.
   A algebra
   B alphabet
   C autograph
   D pharmacy

4 Phyllis wants to know who invented ___.
   A rough
   B elephants
   C graphs
   D laughter

Harcourt

Name _____

Desert Animals

Write one sentence in each box below to show what you learned about desert animals.

Pages 182–183

What surprises does the desert hold?

Pages 184–186

What might you find if you look closely?

Pages 187–188

What other creatures make their homes in the desert?

Use the information above to write a one-sentence summary of the selection.

_____

_____

_____

Elements of Nonfiction: Text Structure

Read the paragraphs. Then answer the questions.

Rodeo Week

Every year, our town has Rodeo Week. On Monday, the cowhands arrive. On Tuesday, the rodeo events begin. The big event on Wednesday is bronco busting. Thursday is the day for children's races and games. Rodeo Week ends with a square dance on Friday.

Summer Vacation

During summer vacation, my life stays the same in some ways and changes in other ways. I still get to spend time with my friends, but I see them at day camp instead of at school. Instead of reading schoolbooks, I read mystery stories. During summer vacation, I still have to help around the house. I have more free time, though, because I don't have homework.

1. In what kind of text structure are events told in time order? _____

_____

2. What kind of text structure shows how things are alike and different?

3. What kind of text structure does "Rodeo Week" have? _____

_____

4. What kind of text structure does "Summer Vacation" have? _____

_____

Fluency Builder

undoubtedly	know	Heather
loathe	little	dread
certainty	through	sleepyhead
protruded	wasn't	sweater
indifferent	food	breakfast
sulkily	pulled	ready
heartily	said	

1. Heather woke / with a feeling / of dread.

2. "I just know / I'm going to loathe / school here," / she told herself / with certainty.

3. "Rise and shine, / sleepyhead!" / her mother / called out / heartily.

4. "Oh, Mom!" / Heather said / sulkily.

5. She pulled on / her sweater / as she got ready / for school.

6. Her cat / had finished washing himself, / but a little tip of pink / still protruded / from his mouth.

7. Undoubtedly / she would make it / through the day, / but she wasn't / looking forward to it.

8. Heather / normally enjoyed breakfast, / but today / she felt indifferent / to food.

Name _____

School Days

Read the story. Circle all the words that have the vowel sound that you hear in *head* spelled *ea*.

After breakfast Rick and Yoshi packed for a picnic.
"I'm making healthful sandwiches," said Rick.
Yoshi said, "Don't forget the gingerbread cake!"
The boys hiked up a hill to a grassy meadow. When they got to the top, they were out of breath and sweating.
"This looks like a good spot," Rick said. He spread out a blanket on the grass.
Yoshi looked at the sky. Dark clouds were coming closer.
"The weather is going to be dreadful," Yoshi said. "I don't think we'll have time to finish all of our lunch before it rains. Should we have the sandwiches or the gingerbread cake first?"
The boys smiled at one another. "The cake!" they said.

Circle and write the word that best completes each sentence.

1. The boys made sandwiches after _____.
   dinner   headlights   breakfast

2. Yoshi reminded Rick to pack the _____ cake.
   headphones   gingerbread   treasure

3. A _____ was at the top of the hill.
   thread   meadow   shortbread

4. The boys were _____ after the hike.
   breathless   helpless   ready

5. Rick _____ out a blanket on the grass.
   spread   unread   red

6. Yoshi said the weather was going to be _____.
   perfect   healthy   dreadful

School Days

Complete each box below to summarize the selection. Be sure to write the events in the correct order.

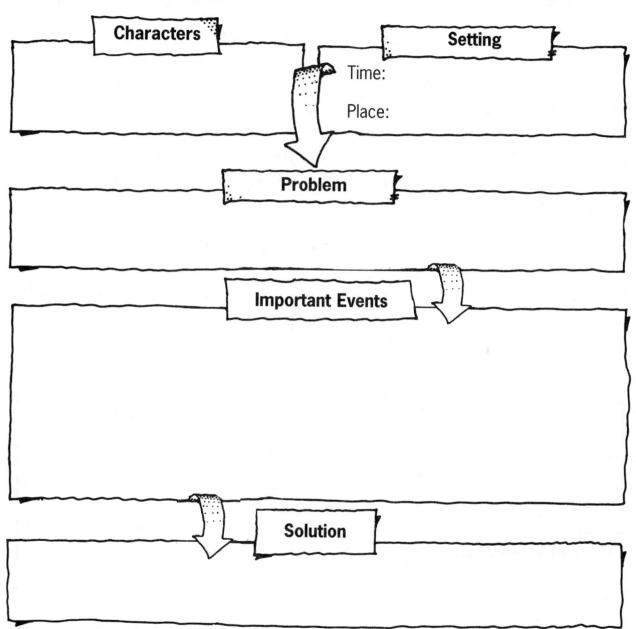

Characters

Setting

Time:

Place:

Problem

Important Events

Solution

Use the story map above to write a one-sentence summary of the story.

Name _____

Author's Purpose

Read each paragraph. Think about the author's purpose for writing and his or her perspective. Then fill in the chart.

Don't Forget Your Breakfast

Eating a healthy breakfast is a good way to start your day. A healthful breakfast gives you energy. When you eat something like cereal with milk and fruit, you already have a good start on getting the vitamins and minerals you need for the day. If you don't eat a healthful breakfast, you may feel tired and grumpy. The few minutes you spend eating breakfast will pay off all day long. Start your day with a good breakfast.

German Shepherds

The German shepherd is a very smart dog. German shepherds can be trained to be police dogs. They can also be trained to help people. German shepherds are often used as guide dogs for the blind and as search-and-rescue dogs.

Title	Purpose	Perspective
Don't Forget Your Breakfast		
German Shepherds		

Harcourt

Fluency Builder

culture	years	would
chile	our	smell
mesquite	where	ground
barbecue	music	eight
accordion	know	neighbors
confetti	someone	their
	air	steaks

1. My name is / Roberto / and this is a story / about when I was eight years old.

2. My grandparents / traveled from a small town / where they know / all their neighbors.

3. Our Mexican culture / is important to us, / so we speak Spanish / at home.

4. My mother / always puts / an extra chile pepper / on the table / for my father.

5. My parents / told us / about the celebrations / they had in Mexico.

6. Someone / would play music / on an accordion.

7. The smell / of burning mesquite / filled the night air / as people / put steaks on the grill / to barbecue.

8. Only / the colorful confetti / on the ground / showed that / a celebration / had taken place.

When I Was Eight

Circle and write the word that answers each riddle.

1. I have the vowel sound heard in *weigh*.
   I am a number. What am I?

   _____

   ten   eight   main

2. I have the vowel sound heard in *break*.
   I am a food. What am I?

   _____

   steak   rake   snack

3. I have the vowel sound heard in *neigh*.
   People ride in me on the snow. What am I?

   sled   sleigh   sail

4. I have the same vowel sound as in *vein*.
   You put me on a horse. What am I?

   saddle   mane   reins

5. I have the same vowel sound as in *weigh*.
   I live on your street. What am I?

   _____

   neighbor   lane   home

6. I have the same vowel sound as in *neigh*.
   You use a scale to find me. What am I?

   _____

   frame   weight   size

   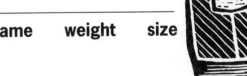

7. I have the vowel sound heard in *break*.
   I mean "very, very good." What am I?

   _____

   best   same   great

8. I have the vowel sound heard in *rein*.
   I am inside your body. What am I?

   _____

   vein   tape   ear

9. I have the vowel sound heard in *weigh*.
   I am a kind of train. What am I?

   _____

   fast   brake   freight

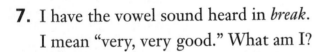

When I Was Eight

Complete the sequence chart about "When I Was Eight." Write a sentence in each box. The first one has been done for you.

**Event 1
(pages 198–199):**

When Junior was eight years old, his grandparents came from Mexico to stay with his family for a month.

**Event 2
(pages 200–201):**

**Event 3
(page 202):**

**Event 4
(pages 203–204):**

Now use the information from the boxes to write a one-sentence summary of the selection.

_____

_____

_____

_____

Sequence

Read the paragraph. Fill in the chart to show the sequence of events.

Every January my grandmother sends out invitations to our family reunion. On reunion day in June, we all meet at someone's house. Right away the cousins start a baseball game. Then we have a big picnic dinner. After dinner we name the oldest relative king or queen of the reunion. Before we leave, we decide where next year's reunion will be.

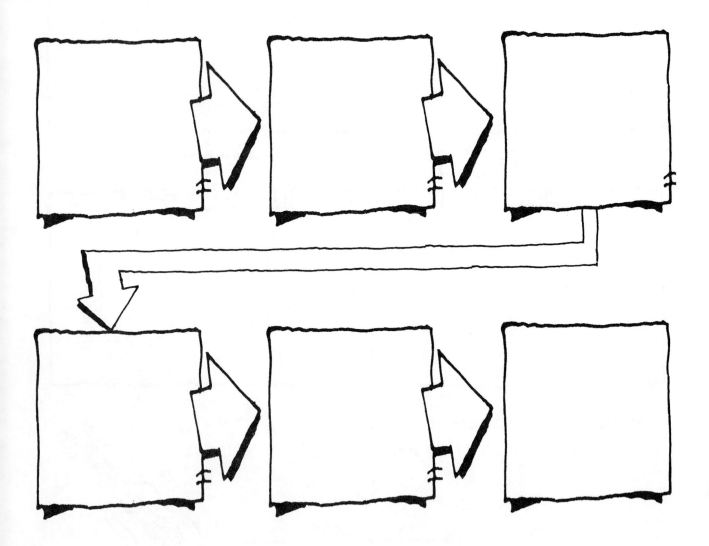

Harcourt

Fluency Builder

abandoned	knew	firmly
profitable	work	breathless
beckons	over	comfortable
fares	could	quickly
rugged	were	hopeful
multicultural	used	beautiful
	make	
	out	

1. In the 1840s, / only rich people / could travel / to California by ship / as the fares were high.

2. James Marshall knew / there would be / few comforts there, / but he was rugged / and used to hard work.

3. Marshall was / firmly convinced / that the sawmill would / make his fortune.

4. Breathless, / he quickly lifted / the beautiful, / shiny stone / out of the water.

5. John Sutter was sure / the stones were gold, / but he wasn't comfortable / about the discovery.

6. The mill / was going to be / far more profitable / than a few small / gold stones.

7. Hopeful people / came from all over / with only one thing / in mind— / getting rich!

8. Sailors / abandoned their ships / and made their way / inland.

9. They made / California / a multicultural state / that today beckons travelers / from around the world.

The West Beckons

Read the story. Circle each word that ends with one of these suffixes:
-ly, -ful, -able, -less.

Sadie is a playful puppy. When she thinks someone is having fun, she quickly joins in. Sadie is agreeable no matter what the game. Even if it is pointless, she will happily play.

One day a large truck slowly pulled up at the house next to Sadie's. Two cheerful movers got out of the truck and began to remove boxes. They were very careful with the first box.

Sadie thought it was a game, so she eagerly joined in. The movers were helpless. Sadie was unstoppable. Soon the lamp in the box was worthless.

Circle and write the word that best completes each sentence.

1. Sadie is a _____ puppy.
       painful   movable   playful

2. She is _____ to any kind of game.
      agreeable   avoidable   rapidly

3. A large truck _____ pulled up next door.
       wasteful   equally   slowly

4. The movers were very_____ with the boxes.
       careful   heartless   wonderful

5. When Sadie joined in, they were _____ to stop her.
       helpless   pointless   blamable

6. Soon the lamp that was in the box was _____.
       skillful   restless   worthless

The West Beckons

Write one or two sentences in each box below
to tell what you know about James Marshall
and the gold rush.

Pages 206–207

Why did James Marshall travel to California, and what did he hope to do
once he got there?

Page 208–209

What happened after Marshall discovered gold?

Pages 210–211

What effect did the gold rush have on California?

Use the information above to write a one-sentence summary of the selection.

_____

_____

Harcourt

Fact and Opinion

Read the paragraph. In the chart below, write examples of fact and opinion statements from the paragraph.

In my opinion, my little sister is a pest. Sometimes she follows me around for hours. She often asks to play with my friends when they come over. If I say "no," she cries. Usually I let her play. Sometimes I think it's fun to be with her. One time we pretended she was a baby bear and I was a daddy bear. I pretended to growl and snap at people who got near her. My sister said she loved that game. I thought it was fun, too.

	Characteristics	**Examples from the Paragraph**
Facts		
Opinions		

Harcourt

Fluency Builder

pioneer	that	tough
fertile	world	rough
harmony	days	though
arbor	named	through
possibilities	gold	
believed	find	
beautiful	found	
country	two	

1. The first Americans believed / that the mountain / kept their world / in harmony.

2. It took Zebulon Pike / and his crew / two tough days / to climb partway / up the mountain.

3. Even though / Pike never completed / the rough climb / to the top, / mapmakers named the mountain / Pikes Peak.

4. Stephen Long did make it / to the top, / and he saw a place / of endless possibilities.

5. When gold was discovered / on Pikes Peak, / the news spread / through busy cities / and shady country arbors.

6. Pioneers came / to Pikes Peak / hoping to find gold.

7. Rather than gold, / most people found / only a fertile landscape.

8. Katharine Lee Bates wrote / "America the Beautiful" / while looking out / from the top / of Pikes Peak.

Harcourt

Purple Mountain Majesty

Read the sentences and look at the picture. Follow the directions.

1. Ben smelled the baking dough. Add more lines to show the dough's aroma.
2. Ben brought three apples to the table. Add the apples to his bowl.
3. Ben thought about lunch. Draw in the bubble what he thought about.
4. Ben's wife had bought flowers. Add the flowers to the vase on the table.
5. Kim ate a doughnut. Draw the doughnut in her hand.
6. It is tough to play with a yo-yo while eating! Draw Kim's yo-yo.
7. There were enough plates for three people. Add the plates to the table.
8. The cat chased a mouse. Draw the mouse running through the room.
9. Two birds fought over some birdseed on the windowsill. Draw the birdseed.
10. The pinecone on the windowsill was rough on the outside. Draw the pinecone.

Now circle the words that have the *ough* letter pattern.

Harcourt

Purple Mountain Majesty

Write one or two sentences in each box below to show what you have learned about the history of Pikes Peak.

Pages 214–215

Main Idea:

Pages 216–217

Main Idea:

Pages 218–219

Main Idea:

Write a one-sentence summary of the selection.

_____

_____

_____

Harcourt

Word Relationships

Read this paragraph.

   Jenny had a nice bowl to sell. She decided to write an ad for the newspaper. By the time Jenny finished her ad, it was almost time for the newspaper office to close. She ran there so quickly that she came close to fainting. Jenny walked up the stairs to the office. The editor said he would add up the cost of an ad. It turned out that the price was very inexpensive. Jenny had enough money left over to bowl and go for pizza with her friends.

Read the list of word relationships in the column at the left. Then write examples from the paragraph in the column on the right.

How Words Are Related	Examples from the Paragraph
Synonyms: Words that have similar meanings	
Antonyms: Words that have opposite meanings	
Homophones: Words that sound the same but have different spellings and meanings	
Homographs: Words that are spelled the same but have different meanings and pronunciations	
Multiple-meaning word: Word that has more than one meaning	

Harcourt

Fluency Builder

bellowing	that	untamed
softhearted	for	impolite
ration	any	disagreeable
tragedy	use	impossible
fateful	when	nonsense
gadgets	wanted	unhappy
	who	
	from	

1. Pecos Bill was softhearted / toward the coyotes / that raised him.

2. Texas became / too calm / for the untamed spirit / of Pecos Bill.

3. Bill didn't use any gadgets / when he jumped on a rattler / of impossible size / and tied it into knots.

4. Bill was bellowing, / "Enough of this nonsense!"

5. Pecos Bill wanted cowboys / who were rough, / tough, / untamed, / impolite, / and disagreeable.

6. The wildcat nearly met / with tragedy / for trying to chew off / Bill's head.

7. Bill asked / for a ration / of grub / from the cowboys.

8. The unhappy cowpokes knew / that this was a fateful moment / for them.

An American Legend

Read the story, and circle all the words that have one of the following prefixes: *un-, re-, dis-, im-, non-,* or *pre-*.

Amaya and her family are at the airport. They are waiting to board their nonstop flight to New York. Amaya is unhappy because she forgot to pack a book to read. Her father disappears for a little while and comes back with a present for Amaya. She unwraps it and finds a book about prehistoric animals inside! Pleased, she hugs her father and begins to read.

"Would anyone like a drink?" asks Amaya's mom.

"I'd like some nonfat milk," says Amaya's father.

"I'd like a fruit drink," says Amaya.

Her mother goes to get the drinks. When she reappears, she holds three cartons of milk. "I'm sorry, Amaya," she says. "It was impossible to find a fruit drink. But I bought you an apple to go with your milk."

"Thank you, Mom!" says Amaya.

Now write the word with a prefix from above that best completes each sentence. Use each word only once.

1. It is _____ for Amaya's mom to find a fruit drink.

2. When Amaya _____ her present, she finds a book inside.

3. A _____ flight does not stop anywhere along the way.

4. Amaya is _____ because she forgot a book for her trip.

5. She likes to read about _____ animals.

6. Amaya's dad likes _____ milk.

7. Amaya's mom _____ after being away for a short time.

8. Amaya's unhappiness _____ when she finds the book.

An American Legend

Complete the chart about "An American Legend." Write a sentence or two in each box. The first has been done for you.

Main Idea (pages 222–223):

After having done many incredible things in Texas, Pecos Bill decides it is time to head west. He goes to New Mexico to set up a new ranch.

Main Idea (pages 224–225):

Main Idea (page 227):

Main Idea (page 228):

Now use the information from the boxes above to write a one-sentence summary of the selection.

_____

_____

_____

Harcourt

Name _____

Fact and Opinion

Read this paragraph. Think about which statements are fact and which are opinion.

My school is called Eleanor Roosevelt Elementary. It has classrooms for kindergarten through fifth grade. E. R. is the greatest school in the district! We have a cafeteria, a library, and a computer room. The computer room is the best. The teachers at my school are really, really nice. Our principal visits classes during the day and sometimes even eats lunch with us.

Read the statements below. Mark an *X* in the Fact column if the statement is a fact. Mark an *X* in the Opinion column if the statement is an opinion.

Statement	Fact	Opinion
1. My school is called Eleanor Roosevelt Elementary.		
2. E. R. is the greatest school in the district!		
3. We have a cafeteria, a library, and a computer room.		
4. The computer room is the best.		
5. The teachers at my school are really, really nice.		
6. Our principal visits classes during the day and sometimes even eats lunch with us.		

Harcourt

Fluency Builder

carnivorous	bat	notion
boggiest	into	concentration
chemicals	sometimes	solution
dissolve	have	direction
accidentally	days	motion
fertilizer	eyes	
victim	help	
	down	

1. Brown Bat heads / in the direction / of the boggiest marshes / to hunt.

2. Brown Bat uses / a flipping motion / to toss mosquitoes / into his mouth.

3. Fertilizers / and chemicals / are sometimes stored / in garden sheds.

4. The bolas spider / uses great skill / and concentration / to catch moths.

5. The moths have / no notion / that they / are being watched.

6. There are days / when a bolas spider / accidentally misses with his bolas.

7. The bolas spider injects a solution / to dissolve his bug roll-up.

8. The praying mantis has five eyes / that help him watch / for victims.

9. All of these carnivorous creatures / help keep down / the insect population.

Harcourt

Bug Catchers

Mark the letter in front of the sentence that tells about the picture.

1 **A** It is the end of January.
  B It is time for summer vacation.
  C It is time for winter hibernation.
  D This is a new invention.

2 **A** Boris wants to go to the seashore.
  B Boris tells how to add fractions.
  C Boris will take some of his possessions.
  D Boris talks about possible destinations.

3 **A** Stella does not like road construction.
  B Stella thinks there is too much pollution.
  C Stella likes this situation very much.
  D Stella says there is a lot of relaxation.

4 **A** Boris has a great solution.
  B Boris will go to the city alone.
  C Boris ends the conversation.
  D Boris tries long division.

5 **A** He will watch whale migration.
  B He is watching television.
  C He suggests jungle exploration.
  D He suggests making a donation.

6 **A** They sail away on their vacation.
  B They go to the train station.
  C They fly to their destination.
  D They go into hibernation.

Bug Catchers

Write one or two sentences in each box
to show how different creatures catch bugs.

Pages 230–231

How do brown bats catch bugs?

Pages 232–233

How do bolas spiders catch bugs?

Pages 234–236

How do praying mantises catch bugs?

Use the information above to write a one-sentence summary of
the selection.

_____

_____

Word Relationships

Read this paragraph.

The day was hot, although it had been cool this morning. I used my hat to fan my face. At last, it was my turn up at bat. I watched the pitcher turn toward me. He threw the ball as I raised my bat. The ball whizzed through the air. Crack! I hit the ball as hard as I could. Every fan cheered and screamed. We would win the game!

Read the list of word relationships in the column on the left. Write sentences from the paragraph that are examples in the column on the right.

How Words Are Related	Examples from the Paragraph
Synonyms	
Antonyms	
Homophones	
Multiple-meaning words	

Harcourt

Fluency Builder

transformed   new   classmates
investigate   across   soccer
enthusiastically   and   writing
decor   may   baseball
apparently   into   interrupted
corridor   get   advantages
    future

1. Paul is writing / to his future classmate / to investigate / what his new school / will be like.

2. Apparently / the moose Paul came across / was not familiar / with humans.

3. The decor / of Paul's classroom / and corridor / is very similar / to Ricardo's classroom.

4. Ricardo may be sent / to the states / and transformed / into a Californian.

5. Ricardo enthusiastically / tells Paul / about the Spanish World Cup / soccer team.

6. Paul will need / to teach Ricardo / about baseball.

7. Air Force kids / get their plans interrupted / a lot.

8. Being an Air Force kid / has its advantages.

Air Force Kids

Name _____

Circle and write the word that makes the sentence tell about the picture.

1. Wilbur and Judy Morris live in a big

_____.

city   foundry   parlor

2. From time to time they enjoy camping

in the _____.

seashore   wilderness   cinema

3. First, they go to the _____

to get supplies. **market**   **palace**   **program**

4. They put their _____ in backpacks.

finches   equipment   bubbles

5. They hike up a _____

corner   gentle   pinch

slope for several hours.

6. They pass through a meadow full of

colorful _____.

flashes   flowers   starlings

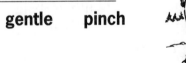

7. They find a _____

celebrate   forward   perfect

place to make their camp.

Now draw a line between the syllables of each word you wrote.

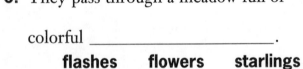

Harcourt

Air Force Kids

Write one or two sentences in each box to tell what you learned about Ricardo and Paul in "Air Force Kids."

Pages 238–239

What did you learn about where the characters live?

Pages 240–241

What else did you learn about each character?

Pages 242–243

What does Ricardo find out in these pages?

Use the information above to write a one-sentence summary of the selection.

_____

_____

_____

Author's Purpose

Read the paragraph and think about the author's purpose. Then fill in the chart below. List the details that helped you determine the author's purpose.

Tarantulas are members of the spider family. Tarantulas have eight legs. Their legs and bodies are covered in hair. Tarantulas do not spin webs. They capture their prey by chasing it. Tarantulas feed mainly on insects, but they have been known to eat small frogs, toads, and mice. The bite of the tarantula is not dangerous to humans, but many people are afraid of them.

Author's Purpose

Details

Do you think the author thinks that tarantulas are interesting, boring, or dangerous? Why?

_____

_____

_____

Harcourt